ANTIQUE GLASS

for pleasure and investment

ANTIQUE GLASS

for pleasure
and investment

GEOFFREY WILLS

JOHN GIFFORD · LONDON

© 1970 Geoffrey Wills

First published 1971 by
John Gifford Ltd
125 Charing Cross Road
London WC2

SBN 70710222 7

Text printed in Great Britain
by Butler & Tanner Ltd
Frome and London

Acknowledgements

The author is grateful to the undermentioned who have allowed the use of photographs of examples in their possession or in their custody:

Bearnes & Waycotts, Torquay: Plate 7.

Christie's, London: Figs. 39, 44, 91.

Delmosne & Son, Ltd., London: Figs. 12, 17, 18, 23, 25, 34, 37, 40, 41, 45–53, 55, 56, 59, 60, 62–5, 72–4, 83, 85, 86, 90, 93–100.

H. L. Douch, Esq.: Fig. 16.

Glass Manufacturers' Federation, London: Figs. 3, 6, 7, 8.

Cecil Higgins Art Gallery, Bedford: Figs. 24, 27.

Mr and Mrs F. W. May: Fig. 92.

Northampton Museums: Figs. 88, 89.

Sotheby's, London: Figs. 11, 13, 19, 21, 22, 28, 57, 84, 87.

County Borough of Torbay, exhibited at Torre Abbey, Torquay: Plates 1–6, 8, 9, 10, 12, 13, 16. Figs. 33, 35, 36, 38, 42, 43, 54, 66–9, 76.

Victoria and Albert Museum, London: Figs. 20, 26, 58, 82.

A. Waugh, Esq.: Fig. 15.

Line-drawings (Figs. 4, 5, 29–32) by Roger D. Penhallurick.

Note

Most of the quotations from old documents have been silently modernised as regards spelling and the use of capital letters.

Preface

The pioneer work on English glass was written by Albert Hartshorne, *Old English Glasses,* published in 1897, and reprinted and issued in New York under the title *Antique Drinking Glasses,* in 1968. When discussing eighteenth-century wine-glasses of which the bowls are engraved with the rose of Sharon, the author added in a footnote:

> When the late Mr Hartshorne [father of the writer] and Mr Albert Way [a well-known expert who died in 1874]—who were, perhaps, the earliest of modern antiquaries to recognise the merits of Old English wine-glasses, and used no others at their tables—made their collections more than half a century ago, 'rose glasses' could be picked up for a shilling, or even sixpence apiece. Those halcyon days are long since gone, and there is no very hopeful prospect now for genuine collectors, who find that a rational pursuit of knowledge is in danger of being sapped or destroyed by a fashionable craze for possession.

Now, more than seventy years after those lines were written, many collectors have come and gone, their carefully selected glasses either dispersed or encased in museums. No doubt each of them made remarks similar to those of Albert Hartshorne, and their followers say the same. Glasses, which are so much more fragile than many other objects, are getting scarcer every day, yet there are always some to be found, and the determined collector is never beaten.

This book has been written to help the beginner by giving him or her an idea of the variety of glass that was made in the past, and perhaps encourage the forming of a collection. It can be done by seeking bargains—which are not always what they were thought to be—or by going to a dealer, preferably one who specialises in the subject. It is costlier to do this, but is invariably more rewarding, both educationally and financially, in the long run.

To train the vital senses of sight and touch, every opportunity should be taken to examine and handle old glass, even merely viewing it through a shop-window or the front of a show-case is enlightening. The study of books and illustrations provides further help, while enthusiasm is indispensable.

Contents

List of Colour Plates

1. Wine-glass with cup bowl above a knop with prunts and a domed foot, all in green metal, the stem of clear glass with opaque twist. About 1755. Height $5\frac{1}{2}$ inches

2. Two wine-glasses with colour-twist stems. About 1765. Heights $6\frac{1}{2}$ and $6\frac{3}{4}$ inches

3. Firing glass with cut bowl and opaque twist stem, height 4$\frac{1}{4}$ inches; wine-glass with gilt-decorated bowl and opaque twist stem, height $6\frac{1}{4}$ inches. Both about 1760

4. Pair of tea canisters with cut decoration, the silver lids and neck mounts hall-marked. 1793. Height $5\frac{1}{4}$ inches

5. Water jug cut with a pattern of relief diamonds and horizontal steps. About 1820. Height $7\frac{3}{4}$ inches

6. Bottle painted in white enamel, the reverse side inscribed: 'How blest is the life of retirement. But yet more blest the Happy pair.' Probably painted by William Beilby. Height $6\frac{1}{4}$ inches

7. Pair of blue glass scent bottles painted in colours and gilt, with metal screw caps over glass stoppers, contained in a shagreen-covered case with red velvet lining. Probably London, about 1770. Height of bottles $1\frac{7}{8}$ inches

8. Water jug of green (bottle) glass with white splashes. Nailsea type, about 1800. Height 10 inches

9. Double (gemmel) flask in striped glass with trailed ornament on the sides and blue mouth rims. Nailsea type, early nineteenth century. Length $8\frac{3}{4}$ inches

10. Wine bottle showing the 'kick' beneath the base. Early eighteenth century.

11. Pair of candlesticks with cut ornament and hanging cut drops. About 1820. Height $6\frac{1}{2}$ inches

12. Blue glass tankard inscribed in gold 'Friendship'. Bristol type, early nineteenth century. Height $4\frac{3}{4}$ inches

13. Pair of green glass decanters and stoppers with gilt decoration. About 1845. Height 14 inches

14. Sweetmeat basket of white, blue and clear glass, the interior inset with spangles. Late nineteenth century. Height 7 inches

15. Oil lamp and heater with ruby (cranberry) glass shade. Late nineteenth century. Overall height $19\frac{1}{2}$ inches

16. Ink bottle with millefiore decoration in base and stopper. Late nineteenth/early twentieth century. Height $3\frac{3}{4}$ inches

List of Black and White Illustrations

List of Black and White Illustrations

List of Black and White Illustrations

List of Black and White Illustrations

List of Black and White Illustrations

1. Composition and Manufacture

Glass is familiarly a transparent, hard, but brittle material, which can also be made translucent, coloured or white, having a history going back to some thousands of years before the birth of Christ. Basically it consists of silica, of which sand and sandstone are largely composed and of which quartz crystals, often nearly colourless and transparent, are an almost pure form. Silica itself can be heated and made to form glass, but as very high temperatures are required for the process it is not practicable on a large scale. A flux, or a material to cause the silica to melt and flow more easily, is essential, and certain alkaline substances perform this task.

It is uncertain who first discovered the essential fluxing agent, or even when and where he lived. Pliny, the Roman writer who lived in the first century A.D., recorded what he knew of its origins in an often-repeated story about some Phoenician mariners. These men were returning from Egypt to Syria with a cargo of natron, a natural form of sodium carbonate found in deposits in the desert about ninety miles to the north-west of Cairo.

They landed for some reason on a shore of the river Belus. below Mount Carmel, where they proposed to cook themselves a meal. However, the beach was a sandy one without any stones on which to rest a cooking-pot above the flames, so one of their number went aboard and brought back some lumps of natron for the purpose. The heat of the fire caused the sand and alkali to fuse and the result was 'a liquid and transparent stream'.

Other writers of the time recorded somewhat similar stories, one of them Flavius Josephus, stating that some of the Children of Israel, not Phoenicians, were concerned in the matter. The whole tale is not nowadays accepted as word-for-word truth, although it is quite possible that some such happening, distorted in detail by much repetition, may have formed its basis.

The earliest known glass material is in the form of a glassy covering, a glaze, on stone beads made in Egypt in about 4,000 B.C. Tinted a bluish-green with the aid of copper, they were made in imitation of turquoise and other natural gems that were so greatly admired in that country. Glass vessels of Egyptian manu-facture date from about 1,500 B.C., and followed naturally from glazed pottery ones. With the uses of sand and natron understood, and ample supplies of both conveniently available, a glass-making industry slowly grew, and spread from there to other parts of the world.

The early Egyptian practice in making bottles and other hollow articles was to form a core-mould of the shape and size of the interior of the article, and fit it to the end of a metal rod. Around this was then wound a string of hot, molten glass until the core, made from a mixture of clay and sand, was covered to suit the craftsman's intentions. The whole article was then gently re-heated so that the strands of glass fused and a more or less smooth surface was gained. When cool, the core was carefully removed by probing and breaking it into fragments.

The small vases made by this method were invariably opaque and in several colours. Successive bands of differently coloured glass were wound on, and sometimes these were shaped into wavy patterns by means of a comb or by teasing them with a pointed in-strument. The resulting articles measure no more than a few inches in height and are only occasionally to be seen outside museums.

Coloured glass beads were also made, often employing the tech-nique later exploited to the full by French nineteenth-century makers of paperweights. Strips of coloured glass were assembled to form a pattern, fused together and then chopped off in suitable lengths. Although it might be put together with large pieces of glass, the fused mass could be heated and attenuated; the pattern

2

remained intact and merely diminished in size as the drawing-out proceeded. A modern analogy is to be seen in the manufacture of peppermint rock, which has 'the name all the way through'.

The art of glass-making duly crossed the Mediterranean. Syrian-made objects were already known in Italy, but the conquering of Egypt by the Romans in 30 B.C. led to the importing of Alexandrian glass and later to immigration by workers from that city. They set up glass-houses in Rome and other parts of the country, and filled both the local demand and that from farther afield in the Empire.

It was just prior to the beginning of the Christian era that there took place a most important development in glass manufacture: the use of a tube for blowing the molten material into hollow shapes. Now, instead of being confined to making small vessels by laboriously winding the glass round a core, it became possible to make pieces of a size limited only by the strength of a man's lungs and his skill at manipulation.

The process was, in practice, employed in two ways. A piece could be blown in a straightforward manner, exactly like blowing a soap-bubble, re-heating it at the mouth of the kiln to keep the glass sufficiently elastic. Or the blob of glass could be blown inside a mould, and any pattern therein would be borne in reverse on the surface of the finished article.

From that time onwards, the changes in technique were largely regarding detail. It was remarked by the late W. B. Honey, after writing at some length on the subject of Roman glass, that he had showed it an attention disproportionate to its quantity. But, he added:

> not only is it important in itself, as showing a complete mastery of all the processes used in later times and a remarkable sense of fitness for purpose and sureness of judgment in their application, but its artistic achievement and example lie behind most subsequent phases of the history of glass-making in Europe.

Although it is not improbable that the Romans set up glass-houses in England, evidence on the point is disputed and until positive finds are made it must be assumed they imported their requirements. A few hundred years later the position was apparently little better, for in the year 731 A.D. the historian, the Venerable Bede, recorded that craftsmen had to be sought in

France to provide windows for the newly built monastery at Wearmouth, Co. Durham. 'This was done', Bede added,

> and they came, and they not only finished the work required, but also taught the English people their handicraft, which was well adapted for enclosing the lanterns of churches and for the vessels required for various uses.

A Frenchman was concerned in the next phase of English glassmaking when, in or about 1226, a man named Laurence and described as *vitrearius* (Latin for 'glass-maker') had established himself at a place called Dyer's Cross, near Chiddingfold, Surrey. Near the border with Sussex, it was a well-wooded area, and it would appear without doubt that Laurence flourished, for in about 1240 he supplied glass, both plain and coloured, for use in the windows of the Abbey being built at Westminster by Henry III.

Laurence settled in an afforested district because he needed an abundance of timber. Wood provided not only the fuel essential for his kiln, but the ashes could be treated simply to make an alkaline flux. There was also sand in the district, although it was not of a high quality for glass-making. In later times it was selected with great care and brought from the Isle of Wight, King's Lynn in Norfolk, or Maidstone, Kent, while in the present century a particularly pure deposit has been found in Scotland.

Other immigrants came to work in the Weald, and there is a record of one called John le Alemayne (*allemagne*: Germany). The French included John le Verrir (*verrier*: glass-maker) son of Laurence, a family named Schurterres, and another named Peytowe. The latter probably hailed from the province of Poitou, and later generations anglicised their surname to Peto. All these men made a greenish-coloured glass, which is not unlike the product of the Romans. While much of their output was flat window-glass, they also made various articles for use in the home and elsewhere. In the latter category were the small vessels with which physicians inspected the urine of their patients, recorded in documents and in the paintings of Flemish artists.

Excavations have been conducted in the areas where these early glass-makers worked, and have produced many fragments of their wares. While some can be identified, most are the subject of conjecture and their original purpose will probably never be decided satisfactorily. One important point to be remembered in connexion with old glass, is that broken pieces, known as *cullet*, were always an ingredient in making up the mixture of sand and alkali.

4

Thus, damaged articles and fragments were valued, and the amount of debris normally associated with, say, a pottery is not likely to be found on the site of a glass-house.

As previously stated, sand together with an alkaline flux makes glass, but such a mixture produces only a soft transparent substance which is soluble in water. This is water-glass, used for fire-proofing fabrics and for preserving eggs. To make true glass the addition of lime, magnesia or alumina is essential, and Pliny's mariners were able to achieve success probably because the sand they used contained sufficient lime in the form of sea shells. It was duly found that pure sand was unsatisfactory, and experiment or chance resulted, in many instances, in the incorporation of small quantities of ordinary lime plus an alkali.

While the Weald glass-makers largely provided their own alkali in the form of potash, the Venetian and other workers in Europe used the ash of a plant known as *barilla*. It grew in Spain, and an Englishman who visited Alicante in 1621 reported on it thus:

This Barilla is a strange kind of vegetable, and it grows nowhere upon the surface of the earth, in that perfection, as here. The Venetians have it hence, and it is a commodity whereby this maritime town doth partly subsist, for it is an ingredient that goes to the making of the best Castile Soap. It grows thus: 'tis a round thick earthy shrub that bears berries like Barbaries, but 'twixt blue and green, it lies close to the ground and when it is ripe they dig it up by the roots, and put it together in cocks, where they leave it dry many days like hay, then they make a pit of a fathom deep in the earth and with an instrument like one of our prongs they take the tuffs and put fire to them and when the flame comes to the berries they melt and come into an azure liquor and fall down into the pit till it be full, then they dam it up, and some days after they open it and find this Barilla-juice turned to a blew stone so hard that it is scarcely malleable.

The plant in question is known as Glasswort (*Salicornia herbacea*), and the hard blue substance resulting from burning it reached the glass-makers in the form of small stones. They were described as 'full of little eyes or holes', the result of air-bubbles trapped in the molten mass. Somewhat similar plants are native to England, but an attempt to grow them or the Glasswort on a commercial scale, which was made in the eighteenth century, did not succeed.

5

The two principal alkalis employed in glass-making: potash and soda (in the form of barilla), had a considerable effect on the finished product. The former made a glass that tended to cool fairly quickly, and the maker therefore had to be nimble at his work. A vessel of potash glass has almost invariably got thick walls, a fact that appealed to the skill and taste of German glass-makers, who were adept at applying cut ornament. This involved grinding away much of the glass, and heavy construction was essential for a successful result.

Soda as a flux gave a comparatively slow-cooling material, which gave the craftsman time in which to blow it as thinly as he wished. The result was a thin-walled, light-weight article, of the type perfected by the Venetians and their followers. It was the Venetians, also, who re-discovered what had been known to the Romans and had subsequently been forgotten: how to ensure a really clear glass, free from the brown and yellow tints produced by iron and other impurities. They found that the addition of a minute quantity of manganese dioxide was an effective de-colour-iser, and occasionally arsenic was used for the same purpose.

By the eighteenth century there was a flourishing glass industry established in England, and from publications of the time it is possible to gain a considerable amount of information about the methods then employed. On the whole they vary little from much that remains in use at the present day, so that a writer on the sub-ject is often at a loss to know whether to pen a description in the past or the present tense.

The industry came from across the English Channel, spread throughout Europe by workers from Venice where the early Syrian and Roman art had taken root. In consequence, the majority of terms used, then as now, were Italian. At least one of them has a place in current slang: the word *gaffer*, the foreman of a gang of workers at a glass furnace, is in everyday use in many trades to describe the 'boss'.

The glass-making furnace was more or less of the form shown in Fig. 1. The fire was kept burning by continuous supplies of fuel, wood being preferred. The art of stoking was to achieve the maxi-mum heat with the minimum of smoke, and the shape of the struc-ture was designed to reflect downwards heat that might otherwise be lost. The reflecting or reverberatory action lent its name to the structure, which is often referred to as a reverberatory oven, kiln or furnace.

Inside it are a number of large and strong pottery jars or

pots, each of which holds molten glass, in some instances glass (or *metal*, as it is termed) of different colours. In front of the pots is a series of working holes or *boccas,* through which the craftsmen insert their iron tools to pick up metal as required. Often there are smaller openings known as *glory-holes*.

The pots, which had to bear being brought up to white heat,

Fig. 1
Men working at a furnace, an eighteenth-century engraving.

stood between 3 and 4 feet in height. Their making was a particular art, and specially selected clays were used for the purpose. If the pots cracked while in use and their contents ran out, the resulting disturbance was likely to be considerable. Work would have to be suspended while the faulty vessel was removed, no easy task as it was still extremely hot, and a fresh container would have to be manœuvred into place. A contemporary description makes this clear:

The worst and roughest work in this art is the changing the pots, when they are worn out or crackt; for that the cover of

7

the great hole of the oven or working hole must be taken off, and the faulty pot taken out, and a new one put in its place through the flames, and that very speedily; the one is done with only hands, and the other is perform'd with iron hooks and forks.

But before they set about this rough work, those who do it clothe themselves in a sort of skins in the shape of a pantaloon, which they make as wet as possible, and which covers

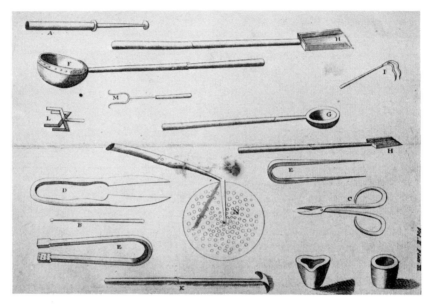

Fig. 2
Glass-makers' tools, an eighteenth-century
engraving.

them all over except the eyes; and for them they make use of glass to see to guide themselves.

And indeed without such a sort of clothing it would be almost impossible to manage this change of the pots, by reason of the long time that it would otherwise take up, and which would be yet more incommoded by the vast and intense heat proceeding from the great mouth of the furnace.

The glass-makers' tools are few in number and simple in design. The engraving of the principal ones reproduced in Fig. 2 was

8

issued in a book published in 1735, and the author of it described them as follows:

The hollow pipe marked A serves to blow the glass; it ought to be of iron, with a little wooden handle at the top. The rod marked B ought to be of iron, but not hollow [the pontil or puntee]; this serves to take up the glass after it is blown, and cut off from the former, so there remains nothing to do to it, but to perfect it. The scissors marked C are those which serve to cut the glass when it comes off from the first hollow iron, when it is given to the master- workman [gaffer].

The shears, marked D serve to cut and shape the great glasses, as also the lesser, to open them and make them more capacious. The instruments marked E serve to finish the work, which the Italians call *Ponteglo, Procello* and *Spiei*.

The great ladle marked F is of iron, the end of the handle being only done over with wood.

The little ladle marked G is also of iron, and covered with wood at the handle; this serves for skimming the metal and taking off the alkalic salt [scum] which swims at the top.

The great and little shovels or peels, marked H, and which are hollow, having the edges turned up all round except at the end, serve only to take up the great glasses.

The less is called the little shovel, and they make use of one like this to draw out the coals and ashes of the furnace where the fire is made.

The hooked fork marked I serves to stir the matter in the pots; it ought to be all of iron except the handle.

The rake marked K is also of iron, and the handle of wood, it serves to stir the matter.

The instrument marked L is for making chamber-pots.

The fork marked M is made also of iron, and the handle of wood; there are of them of several bignesses, they serve to carry the glass-works into the upper oven to cool them.

The great ladle, marked N, is of brass, and hollow, full of holes about the bigness of a pea; its handle towards the bottom is of iron and the top of wood. This ladle serves to take off the alkalic salt.

It may be noticed that almost all the tools are of iron, because molten glass adheres strongly to the metal. It is a property exploited in the art of handling the syrupy substance, which is at a

9

temperature of about 1400° Centigrade. As soon as it begins to cool it becomes no longer workable, and must be held at the furnace mouth (*bocca*) until it is again soft enough to be shaped.

The various stages in the making of a wine-glass require the use of many of the instruments mentioned above. First, the *foot-maker* inserts his blowing-iron into the mouth of the pot, and collects on it sufficient metal with which to form the bowl of the wine-

Fig. 3
Making a wine-glass; cutting off molten metal to form the foot.

glass. Next he walks with the glass-loaded iron to a polished iron slab (*marver*) and twists the rod so that the molten metal on it is shaped and smoothed on the marver.

He now has a more or less egg-shaped lump of glass (a *paraison*) at the end of the rod, and he blows down it so that the 'egg' expands to the required size. He checks that it is correct with the aid of a pair of callipers, and gives the still-loaded rod to an assistant, the *servitor*. The latter has a small lump of glass ready on his pontil, and he applies it to the hollow bulb to form the stem.

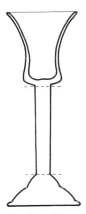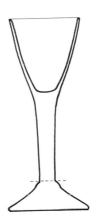

Figs. 4 and 5
(*Left*) Three-part wine-glass and (*right*) two-part wine-glass, the dotted lines indicating the joins.

Fig. 6
Gaffer seated in the chair while making a wine-glass.

11

This is shaped by use of the tools marked E (above), and a repetition of the process adds the foot which is formed with a pair of wooden *clappers* resembling old-fashioned butter-pats.

The foregoing produces a *stuck-shank* glass : one which is in three parts, namely bowl, stem and foot (Fig. 4). Alternatively, the *straw-* or *drawn-stem* glass has the stem drawn out from the bowl, and is thus composed of only two parts (Fig. 5). To make the latter, the servitor has to attach his pontil to the base of the bowl and form the stem from it, and then he adds the foot as before.

Whichever he is making, stuck-shank or straw-stem, the craftsman now has an almost finished glass still attached to the blowing-iron with the stem and foot free. He again takes the callipers and marks where the rim is to be. Then, along comes the servitor with his pontil, a blob of molten glass on the end, and sticks it to the foot of the wine-glass. A pair of pincers with wet jaws is passed round the marked bowl of the glass, and a smart tap causes it to break exactly at the spot so that the blowing-iron can now be put aside.

The wine-glass is now held by its foot on the end of the pontil, and is taken to the bocca to heat its mouth. As soon as the latter is sufficiently hot it is trimmed with a pair of shears, then re-heated to melt and smooth the raw edge. Finally, the bowl is shaped to expand it and produce a familiar wine-glass form, and the foot is broken away from the pontil.

The final action leaves the underside of the foot with a rough scar where it has been snapped off the iron rod ; a scar known as the *pontil-mark*. To prevent this causing the glass to stand unsteadily, the foot was domed slightly and the mark raised above the level of the foot-rim. At a later date the pontil-mark was ground away and the base left smooth. After about 1800 use slowly began to be made of the *gadget* : a rod with a spring-loaded grip at the end. The grip held a glass by its foot, and left no trace of its employment.

The glass is now completely formed, but not ready for sale or for use. It must first be annealed—that is, allowed to cool very slowly. At one time annealing was achieved by placing finished goods above the kiln, and allowing surplus heat from the furnace fire to do the job. From the mid-eighteenth century a special oven, known as a *leer* (German, from *lehr ofen*: empty oven), came into use, and involved putting the articles on a slowly travelling metal tray inside a long tunnel-like kiln. The tray was drawn along very slowly, and over a period of several hours travelled from the hot end to the cool.

Annealing disperses the tensions set up during manufacture. The outer surfaces cool more quickly than the inner when in contact with the air, and internal strains arise. If these are not treated, then the article will be unstable and break apart for no apparent reason. The once-famed Rupert's Drops were good examples of what could occur. They were made by letting small pellets of molten glass fall into water, to produce pear-shaped drops. If these were hit on the fat end there was no result, but if the stem was snapped the whole exploded into powder.

Although the description above refers specifically to the making of wine-glasses, almost all hollow, blown vessels were manufactured in a similar manner. For many of them the gaffer used a *chair*: a bench flanked by two flat arms which give it a resemblance to an arm-chair. Sitting in the chair, he can roll his loaded iron (either blowing-iron or pontil) as it lies across the two arms, taking advantage of centrifugal force to give the molten glass a symmetrical shape.

Pouring molten glass into a patterned simple mould was practised from very early times, but went out of favour with the discovery of the art of blowing. It was revived, however, in the course of the nineteenth century, when the Industrial Revolution began to affect the glass trade as it had already influenced others.

At first, elementary moulds, which formed, say, the gentle fluting round the bases of decanters and jugs, were employed. The article was blown in the normal manner, but instead of 'in the air' the molten metal on the end of the blow-pipe was inserted inside the mould, so that the lower part was impressed with decoration. Then, during the 1820s and 1830s, when cut ornamentation was highly popular, cheap imitations of it were made by blowing into fully patterned moulds. These were made in two or three parts, which hinged or came apart for the finished article to be removed. It was quickly re-assembled and the process repeated.

Wares made in this manner are recognisable because their interiors bear reversed facsimiles of the exterior ornament: where there is a raised bump outside, there will be a depression within— the latter being, incidentally, much less pronounced, but definitely present.

Simple moulding was duly replaced by the process named *press-moulding,* which was first exploited in the United States and then taken up in England. It required a regulated quantity of molten glass to be placed between a patterned mould and a smooth plunger, so that the article was formed when the latter was

13

pressed down to squeeze the hot mass. The result bore an imitation-cut exterior, while the inside was smooth-surfaced in conformity with the plunger.

Press-moulding was limited to the making of open-topped pieces from which the plunger could be withdrawn without diffi-

Fig. 7
Press-moulding, the mould open and the finished article ready for removal.

culty. Plates, dishes, bowls and tumblers were among items suitable for its employment, and which had been made hitherto laboriously by hand. They were all articles for which there was a heavy and continuous demand, and this was further inspired by the low prices at which such mass-produced goods could be sold.

As it left the mould, which was usually hinged to allow for removal, the piece was rough-surfaced and unattractive. A few seconds at the *glory-hole* of the furnace would sufficiently melt away such imperfection, and result in an overall gloss termed a *fire-polish*. At the same time, any raw edges were smoothed, and the article, superficially resembling its hand-made prototype, went to the leer for annealing.

Wine-glass with cup bowl above a knop with prunts and a domed foot, all in green metal, the stem of clear glass with opaque twist. About 1755. Height 5½ inches.

Two wine-glasses with colour-twist stems. About 1765. Heights 6½ and 6¾ inches.

Not only was this a much more efficient way of producing more glass at a cheaper rate, but it also ensured uniformity. It was scarcely possible for one item from the same mould to vary at all from another, and while this may have lessened complaints from the general public it meant the end of the craftsman and his touches of individuality. In future, he was confined to catering for the more wealthy patrons, who admired his handiwork and were prepared to pay extra to own examples of it.

2. Decoration

While plain, clear glass had, and still has, many devotees, a large proportion of the output was given some form of decoration before it reached the market. In fact, in many instances much more time and labour were expended on this work than on the actual making, so it is important to consider the one no less than the other.

As the ancients first used glass in imitation of precious and semi-precious natural stones, it is not surprising that they should have treated both in a similar manner. The lapidaries who worked to shape rock-crystal and other treasured materials used the same technique to shape and decorate glass, and endeavoured to make the finished products indistinguishable from each other. Superficial inspection is often deceptive, but handling usually teaches that the gemstones are much colder to the touch and that the wayward markings of Nature have not been counterfeited with complete success.

Glass-cutting is no more than grinding away surplus portions by means of a revolving wheel, of metal or stone, which is fed with a supply of water and abrasive. A nineteenth-century writer has described in some detail how the process was carried out at a time when it was very fashionable. Grinding wheels were of sandstone or slate, 8 to 10 inches in diameter and $\frac{1}{2}$ to $\frac{3}{4}$ inch in thickness. Wheels for polishing were of much the same size, but made of tin, while others about a foot in diameter, of sheet iron, were for cutting grooves. Small-sized discs of copper were also employed, as were round-ended rods for making hollows. For polishing there were discs made of wood and of cork.

Fig. 8
Cutting.

Of the use of these various devices he wrote as follows:

The cutting of deep indentations and grooves is usually performed by the iron disc with sand and water, which are allowed constantly to trickle down from a wooden hopper placed right over it, and furnished with a wooden stopple or plug at the apex, to regulate by its greater or less looseness the flow of the grinding materials. Finer markings which are to remain without lustre, are made with the small copper discs, emery, and oil. The polishing is effected by the edge

17

of the tin disc, which is from time to time moistened with putty and water. The wooden disc is also employed for this purpose with putty, colcothar, or washed tripoli. For finer delineations, the glass is first traced over with some coloured varnish to guide the hand of the cutter.

In grinding and facetting crystal glass, the deep grooves are first cut, for example the cross lines, with the iron disc and rounded edge, by means of sand and water. That disc is

Fig. 9
Dish cut with diamonds in relief and a serrated edge. About 1820. Length 9 inches.

$\frac{1}{6}$ of an inch thick and 12 inches in diameter. With another iron disc about half an inch thick, and more or less in diameter, according to the curvature of the surface, the grooves may be widened. These roughly cut parts must be next smoothed down with the sandstone disc and water, and then polished with the wooden disc about $\frac{1}{2}$ an inch thick, to whose edge the workman applies, from time to time, a bag of fine linen containing some ground pumice moistened with water. When the cork or wooden disc edged with hat felt is used for polishing, putty or colcothar is applied to it.

18

He added a detail to the effect that 'the above several processes . . . are usually committed to several workmen on the principle of division of labour, so that each may become expert in his department'. Thus, the various types of cutting, and the successive polishings, were the work of specialists in each, and the finished article may well have been held by ten or so expert hands before completion.

It may be mentioned that of the polishing agents putty was not the commonplace mixture of whiting and linseed oil but a very soft powder prepared from calcined tin. Colcothar is known also by the names of Crocus and Jeweller's Rouge, a pink powder which is a chemical product of iron. While Tripoli, sometimes referred to as Rottenstone, was a fine earth found near the North African town of the same name.

Glass was also decorated by the process of enamelling, which in effect is painting it with specially compounded colours fired in a kiln to become imperishable. The powdered colours were ground very finely, mixed with borax to make them set easily and then with a little oil so that they could be applied in a similar manner to ordinary paints. Firing took place in a small muffle furnace of which an engraving published in 1735 is shown in Fig. 10. The letters refer to the parts of the furnace and their uses:

A: space for ashes falling through the grating above.
B: fire.
C: square bars of iron to support the pan of ware.
D: opening through which the pan is filled and emptied.
E: earthenware pan to hold the ware while it bakes.
F: lids, to be cemented in place.

The firing temperature did not have to be anything like as high as that in the reverberatory furnace in which the glass was melted. The heat was, however, fairly critical, for many of the colours would be ruined if they got too hot or would not be permanent if they failed to be hot enough. Test-pieces of glass, each painted with different colours, were put in the kiln and withdrawn from time to time so that progress could be checked. Finally, when it was found that the colours were satisfactorily fired, the articles had to be annealed. This was done either by leaving them in the kiln and letting the fire die down, or by placing them in a leer.

Gilding was applied by two methods. The most durable was to paint on a mixture of ground gold and honey, which was then

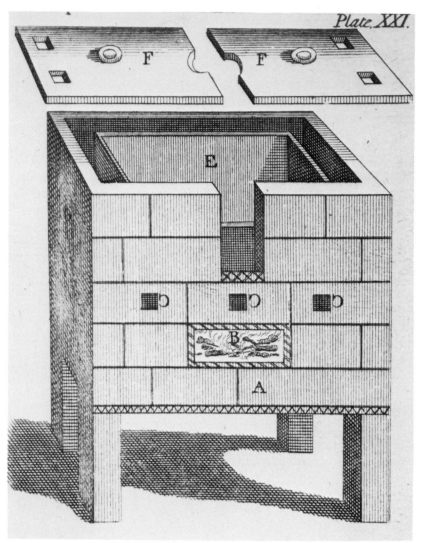

Fig. 10
Eighteenth-century muffle furnace. For
details see page 19.

fired at a low temperature. The result was a matt gold that could be
burnished with an agate or dog's-tooth burnisher so that it
glittered. This type of gilding was by no means everlasting, but
with careful handling a glass bearing it would remain in perfect
condition for a considerable period. Alternatively, thin gold leaf

Fig. 11
Wine-glass, the bowl with decoration in
white enamel. About 1765. Height 7
inches.

could be applied to a coating of varnish, but this would not
withstand much handling and it could not be burnished. When
used in the past, this gilding has very rarely withstood the wear
and tear of the years, and frequently has disappeared almost
without trace.

Colour could also be obtained by using a metal tinted throughout with substances added during preparation of the batch. In
the mid-eighteenth century the following resulted from the addi-
tions indicated, mostly in the form of oxides (manganese was
almost invariably referred to in the past as magnesia):

Red: gold, iron, copper, magnesia or antimony.
Blue: zaffer, oxide of cobalt, or copper.
Yellow: silver, iron, antimony or magnesia.

21

Green: copper, or a mixture of those producing yellow and blue.

Purple: a mixture of those producing red and blue.

Orange: antimony, or a mixture of those producing red and yellow.

Black: zaffer, magnesia, copper or iron, in various combinations.

Fig. 12
Pair of blue glass tea canisters with silver mounts, two silver teaspoons and the silver-mounted tortoiseshell-veneered box to contain them. About 1770.

Also, an opaque white glass, often closely resembling porcelain, could be produced with the addition of oxide of tin, calcined antimony, arsenic, calcined bones, or, under certain conditions, common salt.

Some of the foregoing were known to the Egyptians and Romans, and the latter attained sufficient proficiency to use layers of contrasting colours for an object. Their principal surviving achievement in this respect is the Portland Vase, in the British Museum, which is basically a vase made of blue-black glass overlaid with a coating of opaque white. The latter was then ground

22

away to form the well-known design of mythological figures, popularised by Josiah Wedgwood's copies in jasperware.

The skill of the anonymous Roman craftsmen concerned lay not only in the cutting of the cameo, which was done by grinding as well as by final careful chiselling, but in the successful enveloping of one glass by another. As they were each of different composition, there were problems of expansion and contraction to be overcome. Otherwise the outer layer would long ago have scaled away, or the whole object might have shattered unexpectedly at any time.

The superimposing of one colour on another was in favour from the second quarter of the nineteenth century. Objects made of clear glass were coated with white and then with a further layer of colour, shaped windows being cut through to reveal the first-named. The clear areas were surrounded by bevelled outlines so that a white rim was seen and then the colour on top of it. Often there was further ornament in the form of painted panels of floral and other subjects, while gilding completed the profusion. It is known as *overlay* or *cased* glass.

In the mid-century there were imitations of solid-coloured articles made by giving clear ones a very thin outer layer of colour, the chemical stain usually being ground away to make a pattern. Later, there was a revival of the Roman cameo work, with which a number of men in the Stourbridge area were concerned.

In English glass-making probably the best-known eighteenth-century use of colour, apart from whole-tinted 'Bristol Blue', is in the stems of wine-glasses. The Venetians were extremely adept at the technique of incorporating white and coloured strands in clear glass, and their *vitro di trina* or *a reticelli* remains as famous today as when it was first seen several centuries ago.

The method of making a stem is less complicated than may be thought when looking at an example. The principal requirement was a mould in the shape of a tumbler, of which the inner surface was fluted vertically all round. Rods of opaque white glass were stood in the flutes, and into them was lowered the blow-pipe on which was a blob of clear glass. It was lifted away from the mould with the white rods adhering to it, and was marvered so that the rods were worked into the clear mass. Then with the aid of an assistant it was pulled out into a long rod, being twisted and re-twisted to form the required pattern of lacy threads.

The process could be repeated as often as needed, so that sets of threads could be enclosed inside each other. Some of them might be white and others coloured, so there is no limit to the possible variations of pattern. As with the peppermint rock, mentioned on page 3 in connexion with coloured beads, advantage was taken of the fact that the various components retain their relative positions no matter how much they are extended.

Fig. 13
(*Left and right*) two wine-glasses and (*centre*) a firing-glass with opaque twist stems. About 1760.

An air-twist stem was made in a similar manner, but in place of rods of contrasting colour the effect was obtained by trapping air-bubbles. They were manipulated so as to produce silvery-looking threads, a result sometimes referred to as *mercury-twist*. In both instances, the lengths of rod were cut into pieces a few inches long, ready for joining to bowls and feet.

As an alternative to wheel-engraved decoration, attempts were made from the 1830s onwards to develop etching with acid. The process was similar to that employed in copper-plate etching: the article was covered completely in an acid-resisting wax or varnish, and through this a design was incised so that the glass was exposed. Immersion in a bath of acid resulted in the pattern being eaten away, the depth being controlled by the length of time during which the acid remained in contact.

It was sometimes used in conjunction with wheel-engraving, but by the late nineteenth century was employed alone. Very fine work

Fig. 14
Tumbler etched with a pattern of leaves and butterflies. Late nineteenth century. Height $4\frac{1}{4}$ inches.

could be executed by the method, which has an appearance quite different from that of the wheel. The stiffness that is especially noticeable with curves and is generally observed in cutting is usually absent and a free-flowing line attained.

There have been occasional uses of the point of a diamond for engraving or 'scratching' ornament, but it is a process very rarely used on a commercial scale. In the late sixteenth/early seventeenth century, work of this type was probably executed in London, and a French immigrant, Antony de Lisle, has been named as the artist responsible. The identity of the engraver is perhaps less relevant than the fact that the work gives the glasses it adorns an historic importance (see page 36).

Later, from about 1720 a Dutchman with the English-sounding surname of Greenwood also used a diamond-point. He employed it in a most distinctive manner, mounting the chip of stone in a handle which he then tapped gently with a mallet to make innumerable short lines and dots on the glass surface. The designs thus made are scarcely visible unless the object is held in the correct light, and the work has been described as 'a scarcely perceptible film breathed upon the glass'. Greenwood and other talented Dutch amateurs, of his time and later, frequently employed English glasses for their work (Fig. 15).

There was continuous experiment from the earliest times in order to find more effective and less costly types of decoration. Many did not succeed in becoming popular, others have been forgotten, while a few from the eighteenth and nineteenth centuries are remembered only because patents were granted for them and the records survive.

In this category was a process devised by John Davenport, better known as a potter than a glass-maker, who patented a way of imitating engraving and etching in 1806. The surface of the article to be ornamented was covered in a layer of finely powdered glass, which had been mixed with some substance to make it into a paste. The pattern was formed by scraping off the paste where it was not required, and the article was then put into a kiln to fire and fix the powdered glass. No doubt the mixture was compounded so that it would fuse at a low temperature: a matter requiring distinct care, or the powder would melt into the surface and the craftsman's work be lost.

Examples of Davenport's patented process are rare, and may be recognised by the word PATENT written on a small rectangular label beneath the base. The label was done in the same manner as the rest of the decoration, and in the example in Fig. 16 it can be seen quite clearly to the left of where the stem of the wine-glass joins the foot.

One other Victorian glass-maker merits attention: Apsley Pellatt, who was not only a prominent and successful manufacturer but published a book on the subject in 1849 entitled *Curiosities of Glass Making*. Most of his extensive output is not to be

26

Fig. 15
Newcastle wine-glass, the bowl stipple-
engraved with a diamond point by a
Dutchman, David Wolff (1732–98). About
1770. Height $8\frac{1}{8}$ inches.

distinguished from that of anyone else of the time, but he took out
a patent in 1819 for what are called *sulphides* (alternatively, *cameo
incrustations* or *crystallo ceramies*), which are frequently accredited
to him. This is irrespective of whether they may have been his

27

Fig. 16
Goblet decorated by Davenport's process;
the small label with the word *Patent* is seen
to the left of the base of the stem. Early
nineteenth century. Height 5¼ inches.

Fig. 17
Scent bottle and stopper, with cut
ornament and a sulphide of King George
IV. About 1825. Height about 6 inches.

28

work, that of his imitators, or were made by those he was himself copying. For the idea had been first put into practice some years earlier in France, and he 're-invented' it on the other side of the English Channel.

The sulphides took the form of silvery-looking cameos embedded in clear glass. In the main they were portrait heads of prominent people, whose features are to be found immured in paperweights, decanters, jugs, mugs and other articles. The success of the process depended on the ceramic mixture, of which the cameos were composed, having the same rates of expansion and contraction as the enveloping glass. Also it was necessary for it to be gas-free when heated, otherwise bubbles would rise from it, many would be trapped in the glass for ever and the effect marred.

3. The Start of the Industry

The year 1549 saw the first signs of an earnest attempt to organise a regular glass industry on English soil, one that was on a firm basis and did not have to rely on the casual advent of immigrants. More important, an industry that would supply wares to compete with those of the Venetians or others abroad, who monopolised the market in all but the most everyday articles. Edward VI, son of Henry VIII and a scholarly king, is reputed to have induced eight Venetians to leave their glass-houses on the island of Murano and come to London.

On arrival they were set to work in the City. Seven of them stayed in London until the end of 1551, and the eighth remained until 1569. With the exception of bald mentions that they came and went, we know nothing about the men or their work. No doubt they would have made glass of the type familiar to them in Murano, but none has survived the passage of time.

At about the same date came more Frenchmen, on this occasion from the northern province of Lorraine, whose speciality was the making of sheet glass for windows. The immigrants are of particular interest because their names endured over successive centuries in the districts where they settled. Among them were the

Firing glass with cut bowl and opaque twist stem, height 4½ inches; wine-glass with gilt-decorated bowl and opaque twist stem, height 6¼ inches. Both about 1760.

Pair of tea canisters with cut decoration, the silver lids and neck mounts hall-marked 1793. Height 5¼ inches.

families of Hennezel, later anglicized to Henzey or Ensell; Thisac, to Tyzack; Thiétry, to Tittery; and Houx, to Hoe, Howe or How. They settled eventually in Stourbridge and Newcastle upon Tyne, both of which were close to plentiful supplies of coal.

Coal became essential because the Government had been proposing since the late sixteenth century that wood should no longer be used for firing the furnaces. Centuries of indiscriminate felling by iron-smelters and glass-makers had made noticeable inroads into the nation's timber, which was wanted for a more important purpose. Both for defence and for trade it was essential that the island had plenty of ships, and for their building timber was imperative. Hence those industries that had hitherto burned it with impunity were now coerced with vigour into replacing it with coal.

In 1564, having failed lamentably with the Venetians, the Government subsidised the coming of Cornelius de Lannoy, said to be an alchemist from the Low Countries, for the purpose of imparting his knowledge of glass-making to English workers. Somerset House became his headquarters, but he would seem to have had difficulty with the materials supplied to him and complained also that his pupils were unsatisfactory.

It was noted in a letter written after de Lannoy had arrived, that:

All our glass makers can not fashion him one glass tho' he stood by them to teach them. . . . The potters cannot make him one pot to content him. They know not how to season their stuff [clay] to make the same to sustain the force of his great fires.

Perhaps his standards were impossibly high, or else, as has been suggested, he was simply an impostor; whatever the cause, he faded from the scene three years later.

The next arrival was Jean Carré, a man with businesses in Antwerp and Arras, who had been involved with others in introducing the Lorrainers in 1549. Now, in 1570, he established a group of Venetians, and set them to work in London. It is known that they built their furnace in the hall of the Crutched Friars, near Aldgate, in the City—a building of which the site is commemorated still by a street of the name.

Inevitably the hall caught fire, and one can only wonder that the conflagration did not take place much earlier than it did. On the 4th September 1575, after five years' occupation, the place

31

went up in flames. It was recorded that on that Sunday morning at seven o'clock,

> the crossed friars hall near to the Tower of London burst out in a terrible fire; whereunto the Lord Mayor, and sheriffs with all expedition repaired and practised there all means possible by water buckets, hooks and otherwise to have quenched it.

The simple means of fire-fighting, water by the bucket and not in hoses from hydrants, and poles with hooks to pull down blazing parts, could not hope to do much good. The place contained a great store of wood-fuel, 40,000 billets it was said, and finally only the stone walls remained standing. It was probably sheer good luck that confined the blaze to where it had started, and prevented it becoming a forerunner of the 1666 Great Fire of London.

In the same year as the fire took place, a man who is thought to have been one of Carrés's employees, Jacopo Verzelini, applied to Queen Elizabeth for permission to open a new glass-house. It was to be in Broad Street, still in the City itself and no great distance from the old Crutched Friars premises. On the 15th December 1575 he was granted his Patent, which commenced by stating that

> James Verselyne a Venetian-born inhabiting within our City of London hath to his great costs and charges erected and set up within our said City of London one Furnace and set on work divers and sundry persons for the making of drinking Glasses such as be accustomably made in the town of Murano . . .

It continued by recording that Verzelini would teach his art to Englishmen, that he might practise it for twenty-one years during which no one else might operate a glass-house and that his wares were to be sold 'as good cheape or rather better cheape then the drynkynge Glasses commonly broughte from the Cittie of Morano or other partes of beyond the Seas'. For her part, provided the last ruling was adhered to, the Queen forbade any of her subjects to import glassware during the currency of the Patent.

That Verzelini had established himself at a time when glass was in great demand, especially glass in the Venetian style, is borne out by a well-known passage penned by William Harrison and printed in 1577. He wrote of the fact that because gold and

32

Fig. 18
Goblet engraved with the initials AT RT and dated 1578. The glass attributed to Jacopo Verzelini and the decoration to Antony de Lisle. Height 8⅜ inches.

silver were then plentiful on account of the Spanish expeditions to South America and Mexico, the wealthy preferred imported glassware 'such as do well near match the crystal'. He continued:

The poorest also will have glass if they may; but, sith the Venetian is somewhat too dear for them, they content themselves with such as are made at home of fern and burned stone . . .

Finally, Harrison, in a thoughtful mood, speculated on the finding of a Philosopher's Stone: one that would not only transmute base metal to gold but would make glass malleable. If an article made from this dream substance fell to the ground it would not shatter, but merely be battered out of shape. He prophesied that this would prove only a temporary inconvenience that 'were quickly to be redressed by the hammer'. Four hundred years later we are still seeking such a magical material, but it appears to be as elusive as ever.

Verzelini is the earliest glass-maker working in England of whom there are recorded sufficient particulars for his career to be traced with reasonable certainty. He was born in Venice in 1522, apprenticed to his father, and at the age of twenty-seven was sent to Antwerp to work for one of his countrymen named de Lamé. Two years later, in 1556, he married Elizabeth Vanburen, daughter of a rich Dutch merchant.

He took out British naturalisation papers, and there is no doubt that Verzelini prospered. He lived in Hart Street, not far from Broad Street, and eventually acquired property in Kent. He bought land and farms at Downe, West Wickham, Hayes, Keston, Southborough, Bromley, Farnborough and Westerham, among others, and it is not improbable that timber grown on the estates was sent to London to feed the furnaces. His marriage resulted in a family of two sons, Jacob and Francis, and three daughters, Elizabeth, Katherine and Mary.

The property at Downe, Downe Court, was leased from his father-in-law by Mary's husband, Michael Palmer. In the latter's will there is an interesting mention of some of the contents, rich and colourful fabrics indicating a well-cared-for residence. It told of his

crimson covers and of stools and chairs embroidered with black velvet and green twist; of the cushions of cloth of orisse [?tapestry], being the story of the Samaritan and of Jacob's

34

well; and of those which were grounded with white silk and flowers, being a holly tree full of red berries; and of the grogan [grosgrain] curtains of crimson ingrained, with silk fringe for the windows; and of the ornamental wainscot [panelling] set up on the walls of the manor house.

On 20th January 1606 Verzelini died, was buried at Downe and in the church is still to be seen the memorial brass on which he instructed twenty pounds to be spent. It depicts him with his wife, children, sons-in-law and eldest grandchild, and on it are inscribed the words:

Here lyeth buried Jacob Verzelini Esquire borne in the cittie of Venice and Elizabeth his wife borne in Andwerpe of the ancient houses of Vanburen and Mace who havinge lived together in holye state of matrimonie fortie nine years and fower months departed this mortal lyfc the said Jacob the twentye day of January An°. Dni. 1606 aged LXXXIIII yeares and the said Elizabeth the XXVI daye of October An°. Dni. 1607 aged LXXIII yeares and rest in hope of resurrexion to lyfe eternall.

The home life of the family would appear to have been much less than perfect, if Jacopo's will is anything to judge by. The two sons were each left an annuity of £40, but it was to be paid only on the condition that neither of them should 'vex, sue or molest or rouse of assent to the suing, rousing or molesting of the said Elizabeth their natural mother', or attempt to frustrate the dispositions of the will. To complete the sad picture, the men went to court, Francis suing Jacob, in a suit that dragged on from 1621 to 1652.

There are at the present time nine surviving glass goblets bearing dates between 1577 and 1590 that are attributable to Verzelini's Glass-house. They are as follows:

1577   Initialled RB IB. Now in the Corning Museum of Glass. Corning, N.Y.
1578   Initialled AT RT. Now in the Fitzwilliam Museum, Cambridge (Fig. 18).
              A
1578   Initialled MM Now in the musée de Cluny, Paris.
              DLP
1580   Initialled AF. Now in the Victoria and Albert Museum, London.

1581　Inscribed JOHN JONE DIER. Now as the preceding.
1583　Initialled KY. Now in the Corning Museum of Glass.
1586　Initialled GS. Now in the British Museum, London.
1586　Initialled MP RP. Now in the United States.
1590　Inscribed WENYFRID GEARES. Now as the preceding (Fig. 19).

The nine glasses each have tall wide-mouthed bowls and stand about 8 inches in height. The inscriptions on eight of them were scratched with a diamond-point, which makes a very fine line, and four of them have in addition a band of ornament depicting a hound pursuing a stag and another hound pursuing a unicorn. The 1578 glass at Cluny is engraved with the French *fleur-de-lys,* while the 1581 example bears the arms of Queen Elizabeth and that of 1586 the legend GOD SAVE QUYNE ELISABETH. The ninth glass, that of 1590, is decorated with gilding instead of engraving, and as well as a name shows the arms of the Vintners' Company and the words DIEVX ET MON DROYT (Fig. 19).

Two of the goblets, dated 1583 and 1586, are particularly interesting because they are inscribed with the motto of the London Pewterers' Company: IN GOD IS AL MI TRVST. As these glasses form part of the entire group, sharing similarity of shape, metal and decoration, they are generally considered to have been made at the same glass-house and the engraved ones to have been decorated by the same hand. It is not questioned that all the goblets are genuinely productions of the late sixteenth century, and that their ornamentation is contemporary with manufacture. As Verzelini was the only permitted maker at the time and imports were prohibited by law, there is a strong probability that he made them at Broad Street. A doubt arises from the fact that the legal prohibition was perhaps only partially obeyed, and that a quantity of glass continued to enter the country across the English Channel.

The Pewterers' arms on two of the glasses has led to the whole engraved series being attributed to one man: a Frenchman named Antony de Lisle or de Lysle, who came to England and was in London by March 1582. There, he was recorded as working as an engraver on glass and pewter in the Liberty of St Martin le Grand, and 'without licence from the Pewterers' Company'. Membership of the Company was essential had he established himself elsewhere

36

Fig. 19
Goblet decorated in gilding with the arms of the Vintners' Company, inscribed WENYFRID GEARES and dated 1590. Height 7¼ inches.

in the City of London, but St Martin le Grand and a few other areas were places where craftsmen could work freely out of the jurisdiction of the powerful guilds.

It is likely that de Lysle was in England for a period of some years prior to taking out naturalisation papers in 1582, which would enable the earliest glasses to be included as his handiwork. The 1578 Cluny glass with its *fleur-de-lys* is a possible stumbling block, but it can have been engraved in London and then taken to France, or he may still have been in that country at the time. There is only one glass of earlier date (1577) and it must be remembered that a date on an article, made of glass or any other material, may not have been added in that very year. There is no reason why it should not have been engraved at any time afterwards in order to commemorate an earlier event. Thus, there would appear to be quite strong grounds for attributing all these goblets to Verzelini, and eight of them to de Lysle. At any rate, the theories have remained unchallenged for several decades, and will be accepted as they stand until further evidence one way or the other is forthcoming.

In 1592, Verzelini, who had been operating the Broad Street glass-house for seventeen years, sold the remaining four years of his monopoly and retired to the country. The purchaser was Sir Jerome Bowes, who had had a career as a soldier and diplomat and then became a businessman. Not having the experience of a practical glass-maker, he was concerned solely to organise the industry and ensure it was profitable.

Bowes immediately obtained an extension of the monopoly until 1601, and it would appear that he later renewed it for a further period. Other monopolies, licences or patents were granted to various people, including one to Edward Salter in 1608 for 'the making of all manner of drinking glasses, and other glasses and glass works not prohibited by the former Letters Patent'. It is difficult to imagine what these words can have meant, as very little glassware remained unspecified in Verzelini's original document.

Then followed a series of patents granted to men who were eagerly exploiting ideas to replace wood fuel with coal; a matter which was still receiving considerable attention from the Government. A twenty-one year licence was granted in 1610 to Sir William Slingsby and three other men, for building furnaces in which all kinds of things, metals and ceramics, would be melted by the use of what was then termed 'sea-coal' and 'pit-coal'.

Others followed on the same lines, and a writer of 1612 noted:

greene glass for windows is made as well by pitcoale at Winchester House in Southwark as it is done in other places with much wast and consuming of infinite stores of billettes and other wood-fuell.

Less than a year after Sir William Slingsby had been allowed his patent, Sir Edward Zouch was one of a group of men applying for a licence to make glass wares using only coal. It was granted to him subject to the rights of Slingsby and others, and was to last for twenty-one years provided annual payments of £20 were made to the King and £10 to the Prince of Wales.

In 1615 two events of importance occurred: the use of wood fuel for glass-making was finally prohibited, and another company was formed which included among its members Zouch and others whose patents were thereby incorporated. Among the fresh names was that of Sir Robert Mansell, who had had an adventurous career at sea interrupted in 1613 by a spell in the Marshalsea prison for an alleged political offence. In 1596 he was knighted for the part he played in the sacking of Cadiz and the burning of shipping there, and a score of years later Mansell attained the rank of vice-admiral of England. Obviously a man of considerable character, it was not many years before he had bought out all his partners and acquired for himself the entire monopoly of glass manufacture. This he retained until his death, which took place in or about the year 1656.

While he was still in partnership, Mansell employed a fellow Welshman to act for him abroad. The man was James Howell, who later published a collection of letters mentioning affairs of the day, some of which give information about his travels in connexion with glass-making. While some of the addressees are known to be fictitious, others were real people, and in this category may be included 'Captain Francis Bacon, at the Glass-house in Broad-street'. In fact, in one of the earliest of the letters, Howell wrote:

Had I continued still Steward of the Glass-house in Broad-street, where Captain Francis Bacon hath succeeded me, I should in a short time have melted away to nothing, amongst those hot Venetians, finding myself too green for such a Charge.

In 1618 he wrote outlining what was expected of him and the possibility of making further journeys of the same nature:

The main of my employment is from that gallant Knight, Sir Robert Mansell, who, with my Lord of Pembroke, and divers others of the prime Lords of the Court have got the sole Patent of making all sorts of Glass with pit-coal only, to save those huge proportions of Wood which were consumed formerly in the Glass-furnaces; and this Business being of that nature, that the Workmen are to be had from Italy, and the chief Materials from Spain, France, and other Foreign Countries, there is need of an Agent abroad for this use; (and better than I have offered their service in this kind) so that I believe I shall have employments in all these Countries before I return.

To a friend he recorded parental doubts as to his wisdom in taking such a job:

Your Honourable Uncle Sir Robert Mansell who is now in the Mediterranean hath been very notable to me, and I shall ever acknowledge a good part of my education from. He hath melted vast sums of money in the glass business, a business indeed more proper for a Merchant, than a Courtier. I heard the King should say, that he wondered Robin Mansell being a Sea-man, whereby he hath got so much honour, should fall from Water to Tamper with Fire, which are two contrary Elements; my Father fears that this glass employment will be too brittle a foundation for me to build a Fortune upon, and that Sir Robert being now at my comming back so far at Sea, and his return uncertain: my Father hath advised me to hearten after some other condition.

Apparently he did not heed his father's advice, for a year later he was at Middleburg. From there he wrote to Captain Bacon introducing a potential employee:

The Bearer hereof, is Sigr. Antonio Miotti, who was Master of a Crystal-Glasse furnace here for a long time, and as I have it by good intelligence, he is one of the ablest, and most knowing men, for the guidance of a Glasse-Work in Christendom; Therefore according to my Instructions I send him over, and hope to have done Sir Robert good service thereby.

40

By May 1621 James Howell had reached Venice, and from there he secured two Italians, 'the best Gentlemen-Workmen that ever blew Crystal', who brought with them to England a letter addressed by him to Mansell. In it, Howell gave a description of the city:

I was lately to see the Arsenal [dockyard] of Venice, one of the worthiest things of Christendom; they say there are as many Gallies, and Galleasses of all sorts, belonging to Saint Mare, either in Cours [under construction], at Anchor, in Dock, or upon the Carine [under repair], as there be dayes in the year; here they can build a compleat Gally in half a day . . . There are three hundred people perpetually here at Work, and if one comes young, and grows old in Saint Mares service, he hath a Pension from the State for life . . .

I was, since I came hither, in Murano, a little Island, about the distance of Lambeth from London, where Crystal-Glasse is made, and 'tis a rare sight to see a whole Street, where on the one side there are twenty Furnaces together at work; They say here, that although one should transplant a Glasse-Furnace from Murano to Venice her selfe, or to any other part of the Earth besides, and use the same Materials, the same Workmen, the same Fuel, the self-same Ingredients every way, yet they cannot make Crystal Glasse in that perfection for beauty and lustre, as in Murano.

A couple of days later he wrote that

The art of Glasse-making here is very highly valued; for whosoever be of that profession, are Gentlemen ipso facto.

From Howell's impressions of the Venice shipyards it is clear that he shared the universal opinion of the time that the country was a powerful one. Strategically situated where they were able to control the Mediterranean, the Venetians developed and maintained a large coastal trade which they increased and protected with their navy. Inland, on the continent of Europe, they enjoyed a virtual monopoly of the glass market, which they regulated by strict laws. Employees of the Murano glass-houses were forbidden to leave the country so that the secrecy of manufacture would be retained, but many emigrated over the years and helped to start rival concerns in other lands.

As regards England, Venetians had come in the mid-sixteenth century and now, some seventy years later, Howell was actively recruiting suitable workers. It was obviously much quicker to employ a trained man, than to go through the lengthy and laborious business of devising a glass and the techniques of handling it. For, the Venetians had established themselves in a pre-eminent position, and their productions were widely coveted. The forest glass-makers might supply the everyday needs of the mass of the population, but it was from Venice that anything stylish must be brought.

Venetian products were accepted as the yardstick of fashion, and it was natural for Verzelini and his successors to agree that what they made were 'drinking glasses such as be accustomably made in the town of Murano'. 'Venice glasses' are frequently mentioned in old documents, but this refers to their style and not necessarily to their geographical origin. The latter could have been at any of the many places where absconding Venetians were working: at towns in France and the Low Countries, which were nearer to England and meant shorter and cheaper transport. Although importation was banned at various dates, this would doubtless not have prevented those who wanted foreign ware from having it.

Anything made in England would, therefore, have been in the Venetian fashion, and as far as possible indistinguishable from the real thing. Whether in England or on the mainland of Europe many of the workers had been trained in Murano, and used the techniques employed there as well as closely imitating the shapes and ornament that were second nature to them. At this distance of time, therefore, it must be impossible to tell the London product from that made in Murano, Antwerp or elsewhere, and many a piece labelled 'Venetian' was very probably made at Broad Street.

It is one of the paradoxes in the history of English glass-making that so much is known about the men concerned in the industry in the first half of the seventeenth century, yet no examples of their work would seem to have survived. The well-known 'Barbara Potters' glass in the Victoria and Albert Museum, which is dated 1602 (Fig. 20), is attributable to the time when Sir Jerome Bowes held the monopoly, but for several decades after that there is a complete blank. A very large proportion of the output must have been broken in use at the time or in succeeding years, and a total lack of drawings and paintings depicting specimens ensures our ignorance of what was current.

Of conditions towards the later part of the century we have further information, because of the fortunate preservation in the British Museum of copies of some letters sent by two London

Fig. 20
Tall-stemmed goblet engraved BARBARA
POTTERS and dated 1602. Height 8⅛ inches.

glass-importers to their supplier. The men were John Greene and Michael Measey, who gave their address as The King's Arms, Poultry (a street in the City near the Mansion House); the correspondence covers the years 1667 to 1672 and was sent to Signor Allessio Morelli in Venice.

The first of the letters is dated 12th December 1667, and shows that satisfactory business had been concluded earlier. It runs:

> Sr. Yours of the the 4th November last was received, and we thank you for your ready care (you express) to observe and perform our last order: and Sr. we desire you to take the same care to get us a few more glasses made (and added to our former order and sent with them) according to the number and forms herein expressed: and also to pack up with them 4 dozen speckled enamelled beer glasses and a dozen ditto for wine: the fashions of these we leave to you, only let them be all with feet and most with ears and of good fashion, we suppose this order containing 90 dozen of glasses may be packed in a small chest. Sr. we hope we need not to say any more to you, but to let you know, that we shall credit ourselves so much as to honour your Bill or Bills with punctual payment: which is all at present from
>
> your humble servants
>
> M. M. & J. G.

From a letter written on 28th August of the next year it would appear that things were going less smoothly. The partners acknowledged the receipt of six boxes of glasses, and noted that

> they were right for number according to the factory [invoice], but the beer glasses were something smaller than the patterns and as to the chest No. 5 it was almost quite spoiled; it had received much wet which had rotted the glasses, and we suggest it was wet before it was shipped. For the Master of the ship and all his men do affirm that it did receive no wet since it came into their custody, and therefore we could get no satisfaction from them; the box of enamelled glasses were dear and the worst that ever we had, the colours were very bad and were laid too thick and rough, and pray let these we have now written for be better . . .

None the less, the letter concluded by ordering a further 500 dozen glasses.

A year later there were more complaints of damage to a consignment, and a request that greater care be taken over the packing:

> ...the last we received from you out of the *John & Thomas* and *African* many of the chests were very ill-conditioned; for there was above forty dozen broken and some of the chests had taken water which does stain and rot the glasses, and we could not see how they could take wet after they were shipped for both the ships were in a very good condition, so that we suppose your servants let the chests stand out in the rain after they were packed ...

In spite of the mishap, an order for 600 dozen more glasses was sent together with precise instructions as to their packing. A postcript added:

> That all the drinking glasses be well made of very bright clear and white sound metal and as exactly as possible may be to the forms, for fashion, size and number, and that no other fashions or sorts be sent us but this one pattern only.

Complaints and orders continued in further letters, and the last of the series, dated 30th November 1672, is little different from earlier ones. The writer, John Greene, mentions a previous delivery and tells Morelli:

> ...the last you sent me the metal was indifferent good and clear, but not so sound and strong as they should have been made; for therein lies the excellency of your Venice glasses that they are generally stronger than ours made here, and so not so soon broken.

Then follows an order for

> 120 dozen beer glasses, 90 dozen French wine & 20 dozen of cruets for oil and vinegar, which makes up 230 dozen.

The collection of letter-copies is no more than a fraction of the whole, and in the course of them there are mentions of other importers who were similarly dealing in Venetian goods. The trade must have been a very considerable one, for over the five years Greene and Measey alone were responsible for the purchase of some 2,000 dozen glasses.

English glass of the same time would have approximated as closely as possible in both metal and design to the imported ones, so there is no way of telling the two apart. Quite a few extant glasses correspond more or less to those sketched by the London dealers, but whether they were among the hundreds of dozens sent from Murano to the King's Arms or were copies made in an English glass-house is impossible to determine.

Water jug cut with a pattern of relief diamonds and horizontal steps. About 1820. Height 7¾ inches.

Bottle painted in white enamel, the reverse side inscribed: 'How blest is the life of retirement. But yet more blest the Happy pair'. Probably painted by William Beilby. Height 6¼ inches.

4. George Ravenscroft

After exhausting years of civil strife followed by a period of Puritan austerity, came the restoration of the monarchy. On 29th May 1660 John Evelyn recorded in his diary

> This day his Majestie Charles the Second came to London after a sad and long exile and calamitous suffering both of the King and Church, being 17 yeares. This was also his birthday, and with a triumph of above 20,000 horse and foote, brandishing their swords and shouting with inexpressible joy; the wayes strew'd with flowers, the bells ringing, the streetes hung with tapissry, fountaines running with wine; the Maior, Aldermen, and all the Companies in their liveries, chaines of gold, and banners; Lords and Nobles clad in cloth of silver, gold, and velvet; the windows and balconies all set with ladies; trumpets, music, and myriads of people flocking, even so far as from Rochester, so as they were seven houres in pasing the citty, even from 2 in ye afternoone till 9 at night. I stood in the Strand and beheld it, and bless'd God.

The return of the exiled King from his unhappy sojourn in France led to the extravagance predictable after Cromwell's restraint, and coincided with a widespread surge of scientific inquiry. This was taking place all over Europe, and almost every

47

country was the birthplace of one or more innovations of importance. In France, the Academy of Science united the best brains to the common end; started early in the seventeenth century, it gained the blessing of Louis XIV in 1665 and its members received from him not only funds and pensions but permission to hold their meetings in the Royal library.

A parallel association had been contemplated in England as early as 1616, when it was proposed to found *King James, his Academie or College of Honour,* to include the greatest scholars of the time. It lapsed with the death of the King in 1625, but ten years later, under Charles I, a fresh suggestion was *Minerva's Museum*; a quaintly named body designed for furthering the education of young noblemen. This, too, did not endure, but by 1645 weekly meetings were being held in London by 'divers worthy persons, inquisitive into natural philosophy and other parts of human learning'.

In 1660 the philosophers began to record their meetings, and the first entry in the book notes that Christopher Wren, the architect, delivered a lecture: 'And after the lecture was ended, they did, according to the usual manner, withdraw for mutual converse'. The project duly reached the ears of Charles II, who became a member, and on 15th July 1662 the Royal Society, as it was called, was granted its charter of incorporation.

One of the reasons for the official encouragement received by the various societies was the realisation that inventions frequently benefited a nation as a whole. The discovery of the secrets of porcelain-making in Saxony not only gave the Elector enhanced prestige but considerably helped his exchequer; in place of sending money to the East for Chinese wares, the same thing could be made within the kingdom by local labour from local materials. The bane of modern politicians, the balance of payments, was vitally affected, for Meissen china could be sold to bring in foreign currency and the Elector of Saxony was able to pay his troops.

In England, little was done to compete with Chinese porcelain, except imitate it as skilfully as possible in comparatively coarse pottery. Glass, however, for which large amounts of sterling also went abroad, was a different matter and with the founding of the Royal Society it began to attract increasing attention.

As long ago as 1612 an Italian, Antonio Neri, had published in Florence a book entitled *L'Arte Vetraria,* which dealt with what its title proclaimed, 'the art of glass'. Any Englishman wanting to read it would have to do so in its original tongue, but in 1662, fifty years after it first appeared, a translation was made and printed. *The Art of Glass,* as it was called, was the work of Dr Christopher Merret, a member of the Royal Society and a man who had some practical knowledge of glass-making. Of his reasons for undertaking the work he wrote in some prefatory remarks:

Our own workmen in this Art will be much advantaged by this publication, who have within these twenty years last past much improved themselves (to their great reputation and credit of our nation) insomuch that few foreigners are now left amongst us. And this I rather say because an eminent workman, now a Master, told me most of the skill he had gained was from this true and excellent book (they were his words). And therefore I doubt not 'twill give some light and advantage to our countrymen of that profession, which was my principal aim.

Whether the statement that English glass-makers had 'within these twenty years last past much improved themselves' is a fact may be queried. No doubt the craftsmen grew more competent with practice, but we do not know how they compared with those of other nationalities. Merret's words, 'few foreigners are now left amongst us', must also be read with caution. Those immigrants who stayed would have been absorbed as natural-ized subjects, would have anglicized their names and would quickly have lost external signs of having come from across the Channel.

Such evidence as there is points to glass-making activity having been at a low ebb between 1640 and 1660. Much of the period was that of the Civil War, when Royalists and Cavaliers were battling from one end of the country to the other; hardly con-ditions in which men in general might be expected to show con-cern in any but the most essential matters. In such conditions glass would have continued to have been made, but whether it was improved in any way may be doubted.

Merret's book can be said to mark the commencement of a new vitality in English glass-making, and to have focused on the industry the attention it merited. Robert Boyle, the most eminent experimenter of his time, and other members of the Royal Society were not above showing an interest in, and discussing, a material in which they had more than a purely artistic interest. For their work they required vessels made of glass, which were necessarily reliable as regards strength and clarity, as well as obtainable fairly inexpensively.

With the impetus of the general activity, the Company of Glass-sellers was formed. An attempt to this end had been made in 1635, but without success, and it was not until 25th July 1664 that a charter was granted by Charles II. They were thereby given control of the

art, trade and mystery of grinding, polishing, casing, foiling and finishing of looking glasses and in selling of glasses and looking glasses.

This applied in an area of seven miles round and about the City of London, and also gave them similar powers in respect of hour-glasses, and pots made of stoneware and other kinds of pottery.

Within a few years of their foundation, the Company engaged a man named George Ravenscroft to work for them in producing an improved type of glass. Ravenscroft was born at Hawarden, Flintshire, in 1618, so in 1673, when he began his experiments for the Glass-sellers, he was fifty-five years of age. He is said to have owned ships and to have traded with Venice, so it is not improbable that he acquired a knowledge of glass-making at the same time. Such knowledge, together with an interest in research and acquaintance with London members of the Company, doubtless led to his appointment, but most of his career has so far defied investigation.

The Company set up a glass-house in the Savoy, London, but possibly to ensure greater secrecy opened another farther afield, at Henley-on-Thames, thirty or so miles away from the City. Ravenscroft took into his employment a man named da Costa, an Italian with a knowledge of Muranese methods, and together they laboured to produce a metal that could be made from English ingredients and was at the same time superior to any then imported.

The Venetians used silica in the form of white pebbles, *tarso,* which came from the beds of rivers in Tuscany and elsewhere. To replace them, Ravenscroft tried English flints, which were heated and then ground to make a white powder; hence the still-current term, 'flint-glass'. As this proved difficult to fuse, more potash, which was substituted for barilla, was added, but it resulted in the finished articles becoming crisselled: being covered all over, or in part, by a very fine spider's-web network of internal cracks that made the piece opaque and ruined its appearance.

50

The first intimation the public would have had of the newly devised material was the granting of a patent to George Ravenscroft on 16th May 1674. This stated that

he has attained to the art and manufacture of a particular sort of crystalline glass resembling rock crystal, not formerly

Fig. 21
Three Venetian-style English wine-glasses
of 1685–90. Heights $5\frac{7}{8}$ and $6\frac{7}{8}$ inches.

exercised or used in this our kingdom, and by his great disbursements having so improved the same as thereby to be able to supply both inland and outland markets, whereby the public may be greatly advantaged.

Attention was immediately directed by Ravenscroft to the elimination of crisselling, which in extreme instances might lead to the complete disintegration of an article. Not all the output would necessarily suffer in the same way, but with such a potential defect it was not possible to claim complete success.

51

The answer was found in the addition of lead oxide to the batch in place of some of the potash. While forms of lead had been used in glass-making at earlier dates, it was then employed for the making of decorative objects of small size and not for vessels. Ravenscroft was the first to use it for the latter, and when in addition he replaced flints by sand he had attained his goal.

The Company proudly, and no doubt with relief, announced:

We underwritten do certify and attest that the defect of the flint glasses (which were formerly observed to crissel and decay) hath been redressed several months ago and the glasses since made have proved durable and lasting as any glasses whatsoever. Moreover that the usual trials wherewith the assay of glasses are made have been often reitterated on these new flint glasses with entire success and easy to be done again by anybody, which proofs the former glass would not undergo, besides the distinction of sound discernible by any person whatsoever.

London, the 3 June 1676.

Soon afterwards, a number of glass-sellers, including John Greene, who had earlier been importing goods from Venice, announced:

We underwritten shop-keepers and glass-sellers in and about this city of London do hereby certify and attest to whom it may concern that whereas some of the crystalline or flint glasses formerly made were observed to crissel and spoil; the said defect has been remedied many months ago, and the glasses prove as durable and lasting as any other sort of glasses, there having also been several assays and trials thereof whereby the soundness of glass is usually known. And in witness of the truth we have signed the third day of July, Anno Dom. 1676.

Richard Sadler	Hump: Kilby
John Greene	Thomas Lewin
Jno. Allen	Chris: Seward
Hawly Bischoppe	John Withers

The Company, which had the monopoly of business in glass, was obviously concerned that its new type of glass should be well received by the public. In order to make sure that there was no deception, permission was given to Ravenscroft to mark his improved ware. He then applied to each piece a tiny blob of

52

Fig. 22
Salver, or shallow bowl on a foot, of
slightly crisselled lead glass. About 1680.
Diameter 13¼ inches.

molten glass on which was stamped the head of a raven: taken
from the 'punning' arms of his family.

A year later, there still remained some sales-resistance, and
on 25th October a money-back offer was made in the following
terms:

In pursuance of a former advertisement concerning the
amendment and durability of flint glasses, and for entire
assurance of such as shall buy any marked with the Raven's
Head, either from the glass-house situate in the Savoy on
the riverside, or from shopkeepers who have had them from
the said glass house. It is further offered and declared,
that in case any of the abovesaid glasses shall happen to
crissel or decay (as once they did) they shall be readily changed

Fig. 23
Posset pot with ribbed body, the raven's-
head seal of George Ravenscroft at the
base of the spout. About 1680. Height
about 3 inches.

by the said shopkeepers or at the above said glass-house, or the money returned to content of the party aggrieved, with his charges also, if they have been sent into the country or beyond seas to any remoter parts of the world.

Thus, there would seem to be no doubt that the glass, flint glass or, alternatively, glass of lead, was perfected. The new metal differed considerably from any other that was available. Not only did the lead content make it heavier in the hand, but its presence resulted in a glass that had, in the words of a modern writer,

Fig. 24
Bowl with a ribbed base and folded rim, marked with the seal of George Ravens-croft. About 1680. Diameter 8⅞ inches.

'a light-dispersing character that gave it a remarkable interior fire'. Further, when molten it handled differently from the Venetian, cooling more quickly and being much less amenable to being drawn into the typical detail associated with Muranese work.

The Glass-sellers' Company retained its hold on Ravenscroft and all he produced. Soon after he had been granted his patent, ten of the members signed a letter instructing him in what he should make. It opened by informing him that they now had a new Clerk, Samuel Moore, and continued:

he [Moore] may have the bespeaking of all glasses made at Henley-on-Thames; for that Mr Moore knows what is fitter

54

to be made for the trade both as to fashion and size, than any other there . . .

A further important document, dated 29th May 1677, lists the wares being produced and the prices at which they were chargeable to the Society. Retail prices would have varied from member to member, according to the percentage of profit each demanded. The list reads:

Beer glasses ribbed and plain	7 oz.	1s. 6d.
Clarrett wine glasses of the same	5 oz.	1s. 0d.
Sacke glasses of the same	4 oz.	10d.
Castors of the same	3 oz.	8d.
Brandy glasses of the same	2 oz.	6d.
Beer glasses nipt diamond waies	8 oz.	1s. 8d.
Clarrett glasses of the same	$5\frac{1}{2}$ oz.	1s. 3d.
Sacke glasses of the same	4 oz.	1s. 0d.
Purlee glasses at the same prices as above		
Diamond Crewitts of a pint, ribbed and plain with stoppers to them	9 oz.	2s. 0d.
$\frac{3}{4}$ pint Crewitts of the same sort with stoppers to them	7 oz.	1s. 6d.
$\frac{1}{2}$ pint crewitts of the same sort with stoppers to them	5 oz.	1s. 0d.
Quart ribbed bottles	16 oz.	3s. 0d.
Pint bottles of the same	10 oz.	2s. 0d.
$\frac{1}{2}$ pint bottles of the same	8 oz.	1s. 6d.
$\frac{1}{4}$ pint bottles of the same	5 oz.	1s. 0d.
Quart bottles all over nipt diamond waies	16 oz.	4s. 0d.
Pint bottles of the same sort	10 oz.	2s. 6d.
$\frac{1}{2}$ pint bottles of the same sort	7 oz.	1s. 6d.
Quarterne bottles of the same sort	6 oz.	1s. 3d.

Moreover all covers for drinking or 'sullibub' glasses ribbed and plain shall be delivered at 3s. per lb., diamond and purled all over at 4s. per lb. and extraordinary work or ornament at 5s. per lb. All purled bottles crewitts are to be at the same rates as if they were diamond.

Each of the articles was entirely hand-made and reliance for accuracy of measurement was on the human eye, but surviving specimens more or less match the descriptions. For example, a decanter in the British Museum holds nine-tenths of a pint and

Fig. 25
Decanter, the body partly ribbed and with
a band of trailed ornament. About 1685.
Height about 7 inches.

weighs 11 oz., while a beer glass or tankard, in the Victoria and Albert Museum weighs 6½ oz.

The styles of ornament have been the subject of debate, for it is not definite what 'purlee' might have been. Perhaps it was

Fig. 26
Decanter of purple glass, the neck ribbed and the body with 'nipt diamond waies' ornament. About 1680. Height 6½ inches.

a spelling of 'pearly', meaning covered in small, pearl-like markings, and glasses with their surface dimpled all over are not unknown. It was a type of decoration used in Venice, was copied in England in early seventeenth-century silver, but is not recorded on extant wares of Ravenscroft's time. However, this is not conclusive, as examples with such a finish may well have disappeared during three hundred years.

The term 'ribbed' is still current and needs no explanation. Some of Ravenscroft's marked pieces have raised ribbing, which is not only decorative but gives strength. A variety of it is curved, as opposed to being straight, and in that case is usually referred to as

Fig. 27
Ewer of crisselled lead glass, the body and foot ribbed and Ravenscroft's seal at the lower terminal of the handle. About 1680. Height 9 inches.

'gadrooned'. While Ravenscroft does not use that word, some of his glasses are ornamented with it and it may be assumed that 'ribbing' covered both types.

Finally, 'nipt diamond waies', which is a pretty way of expressing it, refers to raised narrow ribs forming a diamond-shaped lattice effect on the surface of a piece. Again, there are surviving examples of George Ravenscroft's time, and later.

As with everything successful, the glass of lead was quickly imitated. It was in May 1677 that the raven's-head seal began to be

58

used, and although the particular device may not have been forged there were certainly others in use then or soon afterwards. Three examples are known, a posset pot, a goblet and the stem of a goblet, each bearing a seal with the letter 'S' on it, which is conjectured to indicate that they were made at a glass-house in Salisbury Court, off Fleet Street.

Two specimens, the stem of a wine-glass and a posset pot, are sealed with a female figure shooting with a bow; a device thought to have been employed by two men, John Bowles and William Lillington, who had a glass-house at Ratcliff, Southwark, across the river Thames from the others. They made an old-style glass, without the addition of lead, and sealed it to conform with fashion; or was it to deceive buyers into thinking they had an example of Ravenscroft's improved product?

Two further seals are known from printed mentions of their use. In 1683 it was announced in the *London Gazette* that Henry Holden had been appointed glass-maker to King Charles II, and that he had received permission to mark his wares with the Royal arms. Holden had his premises in the Savoy, as did Ravenscroft and then Bishop, but no specimens bearing such a mark have yet come to light.

Equally undiscovered are any of the products of a glass-house at Wapping, in which the Duke of York, brother of the King and later succeeding to the throne as James II, had an interest—doubtless a financial one. It was advertised in the *London Gazette* on 4th December 1684, and announced:

At his Royal Highness's Glass-House near the Hermitage Stairs in Wapping, are to be exposed to Sale all manner of Flint Glasses, and likewise all sorts of Ordinary and Green, with all other Curiosities that can be made of Glass, all the Glasses being marked with a Lion and Coronet to prevent Counterfeits.

A total of about a score of pieces sealed with the raven's head has now been recorded. All have been found during the present century, for when Albert Hartshorne wrote his book *Old English Glasses* in 1897, he knew of them only from documents. Of examples, he wrote: 'None of these sealed Ravenscroft–Costa glasses have been recognised at the present day', and added that the practice of marking with a maker's name went back in time to the Phoenician glass-makers.

George Ravenscroft wrote to the Glass-sellers' Company in

August 1678 giving six months' notice of his intention to retire from working for them. The reason for the action is not known, but as he was then approaching sixty, he possibly felt he had earned a rest. Two years later, in May 1681, he died, being survived for two years more by his wife, Elizabeth, and leaving no children.

Hawley Bishop carried on experimenting at Henley from 1676, and on the demise of Ravenscroft was in charge at the Savoy. Little more detailed information has come to light about the exciting early days of the new glass, which was soon being made in many parts of the country and completely replacing importations. The practice of sealing fell into disuse during the 1680s, so it was current over a total of some dozen years. Probably the rapidly increasing output made it impossible to give each item the extra attention of applying a blob of hot glass and impressing it. Such an operation would be expensive in time and labour, and once the glass was accepted as good and free from crisselling no 'built-in' guarantee was needed.

Back in 1645, Oliver Cromwell had endeavoured to ensure that the glass-makers paid their share of Government costs, and laid a tax on their products at the rate of one shilling for each £1 of value. Just fifty years later, the industry was again remembered, and William III, anxious to raise money to fight the French, taxed flint glass at 20 per cent. The duty was for just five years, but like so many other impositions of the type the period was shortly extended to the indefinite. There was an immediate and loud outcry, with the result that the tax was halved in 1698 and abolished altogether in the year following. It had realised a total of £10,000 per annum while it was levied, so perhaps its contribution to the war effort of the time was not sufficiently outstanding to have made its collection worth while.

Much of what we know about glass-making in the last years of the seventeenth century is due to the industrious efforts of John Houghton. He was a member of the Royal Society from 1680, and published his *Letters for the Improvement of Commerce and Trade*, which were in the form of a series of epistles describing conditions in various industries and trades. In No. 198, dated 15th May 1696, he gave a most interesting list with the locations of all the glass-houses of which he had a knowledge, together with a note of the type of product they made: i.e. flint (lead) glass, bottle glass, ordinary (non-lead) glass, or sheet glass for use in windows. As it is difficult to summarise, it is reprinted here in full:

60

An Account of all the Glass Houses in England & Wales	The several Counties they are in	The Number of Houses	And the Sort of Glass each House makes
In and about London & Southwark		9	For bottles
		2	Looking glass plates
		4	Crown glass & plates
		9	Flint glass & ordinary
Woolwich	Kent	1	Crown glass & plates
		1	Flint glass & ordinary
Isle of Wight	Hampshire	1	Flint glass & ordinary
Topsham, nr. Exeter	Devonshire	1	Bottles
Odd Down, nr. Bath	Somersetshire	1	Bottles
Chellwood		1	Window glass
In and about Bristol		5	Bottles
		1	Bottles & window glass
		3	Flint glass & ordinary
Gloucester	Gloucestershire	3	Bottles
Newnham		2	Bottle Houses
Swansea in Wales	Glamorgan	1	Bottles
Oaken Gate	Shropshire	1	Bottles & window glass
Worcester	Worcestershire	1	Flint, green & ordinary
Coventry	Warwickshire	1	Flint, green & ordinary
Stourbridge	Worcestershire	7	Window glass
		5	Bottles
		5	Flint, green & ordinary
Near Liverpool	Lancashire	1	Flint, green & ordinary
Warrington		1	Window glass
Nottingham	Nottingham	1	Bottles
Awsworth		1	Flint, green & ordinary
Custom More		1	Bottles
Nr. Awsworth		1	Flint, green & ordinary
Nr. Silkstone	Yorkshire	1	Bottles
Nr. Ferrybridge		1	Bottles
		1	Flint, green & ordinary
King's Lynn		1	Bottles
Yarmouth		1	Flint, green & ordinary
		1	Bottles
Newcastle-upon-Tyne	Northumberland	6	Window glass
		4	Bottles
		1	Flint, green & ordinary
	Total	88	

61

John Houghton's list shows that within a matter of twenty years or so of its introduction lead glass was being made at thirteen places. One of them, London, had nine separate manufactories, but the majority only a single one. Vieing with the capital as a centre of production was Stourbridge, with five glass-houses making 'flint, green and ordinary'.

Ravenscroft's marked pieces show that he mostly copied popular Venetian shapes, but in some instances with clumsy-looking results. This was due not so much to a lack of skill on the part of the glass-blowers, but because of the different nature of the metal. The Venetian material, light in weight and blown very thinly, defied close copying in the newly devised lead glass. The latter not

Fig. 28
Ceremonial goblet and cover of Venetian pattern. English lead glass, about 1660. Height 21¼ inches.

Pair of blue glass scent bottles painted in colours and gilt, with metal screw caps over glass stoppers, contained in a shagreen-covered case with red velvet lining. Probably London, about 1770. Height of bottles 1⅞ inches.

Water jug of green (bottle) glass with white splashes. Nailsea type, about 1800. Height 10 inches.

only resisted attempts to blow and tease it into the complex foreign forms, but much of its attractiveness disappeared when this was done. Its principal beauty, its deep luminosity, relied on thicker and heavier shapes than were then popular.

As the turn of the century approached, the public was beginning to appreciate the individuality of their native product. Less and less use was made of foreign models, and the addition of what Ravenscroft called 'extraordinary work or ornament' gradually ceased. In its place, the qualities of the glass itself dictated the forms of finished vessels, which relied more and more on plain surfaces and not on applied tortuous designs of twisted rods.

In assessing surviving glassware of the later seventeenth century, we must consider ourselves fortunate that any specimens remain intact. As it is, there is a surprising amount in view of the delicate nature of their material. No doubt the bigger proportion of the output of the time comprised drinking-glasses for all purposes, and because they were cheap and in daily use they were quickly smashed. The number surviving from the years before 1700 is small. On the other hand, many of the pieces that were comparatively rare and costly in their day, large ceremonial and decorative cups and covers and bowls, have luckily been preserved.

At a glance, the picture presented is of an age when only such grand articles were made, and because commonplace objects have almost completely vanished it may be thought that they never existed. In most instances the fact that they did is known principally from casual references in contemporary documents. Thus in the records of the Myddelton family, of Chirk Castle, Denbighshire, there are the following brief entries in account books:

11th November 1678. Payd Mr Goodwine, of Wrexham, for
6 cristall clarrett glasses 4s., 6 flint large glasses 12s.
20th April 1688. Pd Mr Charles Myddelton, what he pd. for
3 flint glasses at Morton Hall 1s.

There are tens of thousand of similar records in old account books, wills and other documents. They give a very vivid picture of past everyday life, which is usually different from the idea to be gained from the splendid exhibits in museum show-cases.

5. The Eighteenth Century

The greatest proportion of surviving English glassware is in the form of drinking-glasses, and of these the majority of collectable examples date from the eighteenth century. As they were the everyday articles for which the material was ideal, their production was on a large scale to satisfy public demand. Extant examples, numbering many thousands, can only be a fraction of the original output, which must have been truly enormous.

In considering the glasses made over a period of a complete century there are predictably numerous differences to be observed. Not only were they made in various sizes according to the beverage for which they were intended, but styles changed in glassware just the same as they did in the case of silver, furniture and all the other contents of a home. A strong drink, which was taken a small quantity at a time, required a small-bowled glass, and vice versa, while changed habits caused beverages to go in and out of fashion and their particular glasses to follow suit. In the study of the subject, there is as much to be learned about social and economic history as there is about actual glass manufacture.

Dating eighteenth-century glasses relies on a number of points: the pattern of stem, the type of foot, the shape of bowl, and the

64

variety and style of decoration if any is present. It has been explained earlier (page 10) how wine-glasses were made, one at a time, by a craftsman and his assistant; although there must have been sketches or prototypes for the men to copy, there were no moulds and each finished article was different from the next. Such differences were often only very slight, the men would have had wood templates against which to work, but this individuality is not the least of the attractions to present-day collectors. It is all the more noticeable in a twentieth-century world, where almost everything is machine-made to a precision undreamed of in the past.

In 1948 the late E. Barrington Haynes tidied the existing confusion of nomenclature by placing the various parts of wine-glasses in definite categories, sub-dividing them according to

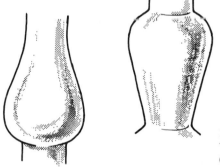

Fig. 29
Wine-glass stems: (*left*) true baluster and (*right*) inverted baluster.

pattern, and it is convenient to follow in his footsteps. The stem is where the greatest variations in pattern are to be found, and the principal ones are the true baluster and the inverted baluster (Figs. 29 and 30). The name comes from that of the blossom of the wild pomegranate, to which the baluster bears a close resemblance in shape. As the form of a wine-glass stem the inverted baluster made an appearance as early as about 1680, but it was some decades before anyone thought of turning it right way up as a change.

The various kinds of knop, which were used in combination with other forms or else on their own, came into fashion after 1690, and of them all the annulated knop (Fig. 30, D) is probably the one most often encountered. Some did not endure for very long, and when glasses of lighter pattern became fashionable the more solid knops ceased to be used. It was the art of the clever craftsman to combine the most suitable elements in the repertoire

65

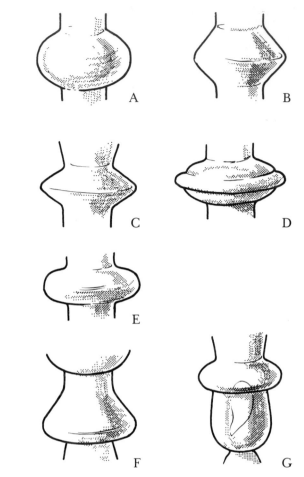

Fig. 30
Wine-glass stems: (A) true knop; (B) angu-
lar knop; (C) bladed knop; (D) annulated
knop; (E) annular knop; (F) drop knop;
and (G) acorn knop.

so as to make a balanced article that would appeal to the eye of the
day, and, inadvertently, to the collectors of the future.

Bowls were somewhat less varied in pattern than stems. The
most popular are those shown in Fig. 31, the round funnel being
the commonest. It began to make an appearance during the
second decade of the eighteenth century, and retained its
popularity throughout.

Finally, the foot, which was the portion showing the least
change. The simple conical is the most common, followed by the

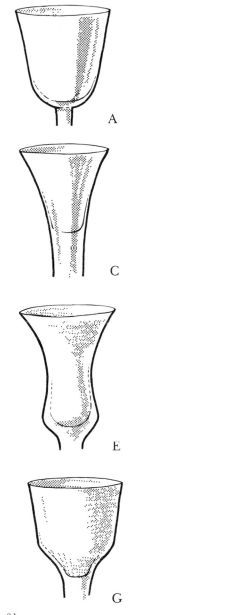
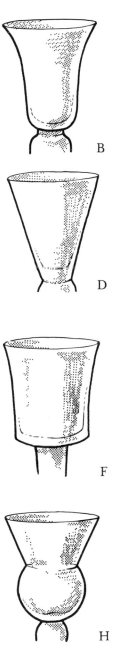

A

B

C

D

E

F

G

H

Fig. 31
Wine-glass bowls: (A) round funnel;
(B) bell; (C) trumpet; (D) conical; (E)
waisted; (F) bucket; (G) ogee; and (H)
thistle.

67

somewhat taller domed type (Fig. 32, A and C). Both served to raise the rough pontil mark above table-level, where it could not cause any damage. Conical and domed feet were either left plain at the edges, or folded under to give added strength where chipping was probable (Fig. 32, B and C). From about 1780, glassmakers ground away the pontil mark, so that the foot could be made much flatter than before.

One other foot that remained popular during much of the century was that of the so-called 'firing-glass'. Examples are squat with short stems and thick, heavy feet (Figs. 13/32, D, and Plate 3. They acquired their name because they were used to give

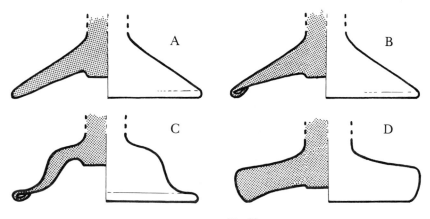

Fig. 32
Wine-glass feet: (A) plain conical; (B) folded conical; (C) domed and folded; and (D) firing.

applause by banging them on the table-top, the noise caused being similar to that of a volley of musketry. Their sturdy construction would appear to have withstood such usage with success, because a surprising number of them have been preserved in good condition. Their heyday was roughly between the years 1730 and 1770.

The foregoing are the principal types of the various features that are likely to be encountered, but one of the interests of glass-collecting is the discovery of something out of the ordinary. Some few are unique, and others are known to have survived only in comparatively small numbers. Among these is the so-called *Silesian stem*, which is of inverted baluster shape and moulded with four, six or eight sides.

Fig. 33
Wine-glass on a moulded Silesian stem
with crowns on the shoulders. About 1715.
Height 6¾ inches.

They were made between about 1715 and 1760, and gained their name because of their introduction at the time George I came to the throne. The German origin of the monarch accounted for many innovations from that country, and among them was the distinctive stem. It was used in Western Germany, in glass-houses in the state of Hesse, but the name 'Silesian', although erroneous, has been applied to it for so long that it is now accepted irrespective of its accuracy.

Fig. 34
A group of wine-glasses showing variously shaped bowls, stems and feet. Early eighteenth century. Average height 7 inches.

The rarer forms of this type of stem are moulded on the shoulder with inscriptions such as *God Save King G,* or the name *George.* Others have the Royal initials *G R.* All will be found referred to sometimes as 'shouldered' or 'moulded', and very few of the inscribed examples are to be found outside museums.

One of the most debatable points in the history of glass is the effect on its manufacture of the imposition of a tax in 1745. The industry had remained free since the repeal in 1699 of William III's duty, but in 1745 the Government of George II required money for the same purpose as its predecessor, to fight the French, and sought it from the glass-makers. They were required to pay at

70

the rate of nine shillings and fourpence on each 112 lb. (hundred-weight) of raw material, and following the path of their Williamite forerunners they immediately protested loudly. They were, however, unable to achieve success, for the Government stood firm and the industry had to carry on and accept the burden.

It has been argued that the effect of the duty was principally to cause the makers to concentrate rather on the decoration of their products, than on the glass itself. Thus, the price paid by the public was more for the labour expended on the ornament, than for the metal and the work of the gaffer and his gang.

This state of affairs did eventually come about, but whether it is attributable to the duty, which was gradually increased as the century progressed, is uncertain. What it probably did was to cause the makers to modify the batch, lessening the quantity of lead oxide, which was weighty, and using more cullet. The latter was untaxed, and its presence up to a proportion of a half, while somewhat influencing the appearance of the finished glass, would not seriously have affected its sale. Certainly, it kept the price down.

Decorated glass began to be popular at about the time George I became King, in 1714. A year afterwards, following lengthy negotiations, the Treaty of Utrecht was signed, and as a result German glass was imported and in time some of the workers came to England. The productions of the latter were not entirely unknown, for as early as 1709 the *London Gazette* had announced:

There is lately brought over a great parcel of very fine German Cut and Carved Glasses, viz. Jellies, Wine and Water Tumblers, Beer and Wine Glasses with Covers, and divers other sorts. The like hath not been exposed to public sale before.

One of the first English cutters was John Akerman, whose name denotes a German origin, and who advertised briefly in 1719:

John Akerman, at the Rose and Crown, Cornhill, continues to sell all sorts of tea, chinaware, plain and diamond cut flint glasses.

The use of the phrase 'continues to sell' can be taken to mean that such glasses were not being offered for the first time. On the other hand, the wording is too vague for basing on it an opinion as to whether he had been offering cut glasses for a matter of days, weeks or even years.

Fig. 35
Wine-glass with cut ornament, the stem
and foot faceted. About 1770. Height
about 7 inches.

Akerman is known to have been a member of the Glass-sellers' Company and to have held various offices in it. After 1746 he moved his business to Fenchurch Street, where his son, Isaac, later carried it on. In spite of this information, we do not know in detail the type of glass he supplied, but certainly he was early in the field as a seller of cut pieces and must have helped to popularise them.

Cutting was executed on the bowls and stems of wine-glasses, and took the form of flat facets or a series of upright flutes. Altern-atively, inscriptions and designs were cut on the wheel, and these occasionally include a date. Dates, however, must generally be treated with caution, as they can have been so placed to com-memorate a past event and do not reliably provide a clue to the style or ornament current at the time.

In the same way, another fashion that came and went in the late seventeenth/early sixteenth century must be regarded with circumspection. The stem of a glass, particularly a large-sized goblet was made hollow, and in a bulge, or *knop,* a silver coin was imprisoned. The date on the coin would doubtless have been specially chosen, but there is no means of knowing whether it was that of the year in which the glass was made. All that can be said is that it cannot have been minted later; and therefore that the glass itself is of the year in question—or later (Fig. 36).

The attractive stems of glasses which are patterned with silvery, coloured or opaque white patterns excite attention, because they are not only pretty but rare and expensive. The silvery *air-twist,* or *mercury-twist,* appeared first in about 1750 and was on the market for about the next twenty years. The opaque white over-lapped it, but did not start until about 1755, and continued to be produced until 1780. The rarest of them, the colour-twist, was made in a number of combinations, usually having white together with red, blue, brown, green and yellow. They can be found singly or with several of them arranged together to make a fascinating lace-like spiral. Colour-twists were current roughly between 1755 and 1775. In all cases, some authorities argue that the periods when each variety was current were longer or shorter than those given, but the above are safe averages and it may well be that some were exceeded by a few years one way or the other.

Glasses were decorated occasionally with gilding: gold leaf applied to varnish, or ground to a powder, mixed with honey and after being applied given a gentle firing in a kiln. The first-named method was not long-lasting and traces of its use have

73

Fig. 36
Tankard with a ribbed handle and part-moulded body; in the base is enclosed a silver coin of 1750. Height 6 inches.

mostly completely gone, but the fired version has proved more permanent. It was used for rims as well as for decorative patterns on bowls, and is rarely seen in completely unworn condition.

Allied to painted gilding is painting in colours, which was fired after the work was completed and is often referred to as *enamelling* (see page 19 and plate 6). It was executed in white and in single or mixed colours, and in the hands of a skilled artist could give charming and lasting results.

No doubt there were many who did such work and whose names remain unknown. One of them, William Beilby, is remembered not only on account of his exceptional talent but because, fortunately, he signed some of his work. Beilby was one of the seven children of a Durham jeweller, who moved with his family to Newcastle upon Tyne in 1760. All the family had artistic leanings and one of them, Ralph, was an engraver who took as an apprentice Thomas Bewick. The latter became an eminent practitioner of the craft and his wood-cuts of birds and animals gained him a lasting fame. He wrote a memoir of his life, which was published in 1862, and in it recorded information about the Beilbys.

From this it is learned that William Beilby, born in 1740, was responsible for glass enamelling, and sometimes he was helped by his sister, Mary, who was born in 1749. Bewick wrote that when he began his apprenticeship, the brother and sister, then aged twenty-seven and eighteen, had 'constant employment of enamel-painting on glass'. As he mentions no others of the family being concerned, it can be assumed that only those two, jointly or individually, were employed at it.

Signed examples bear only the surname, with the exception of a decanter in the Victoria and Albert Museum, which is inscribed *Beilby Junr. pinxit & invt. Ncastle*. The decanter has on it the diamond-scratched date *1762*, which may have been added by someone unconnected with the enamelling, and as Mary was only thirteen in that year, and if it was executed then, she would surely have had little or no part in the work.

Other articles, wine-glasses and goblets among them, are decorated with coats of arms and with small landscapes, some of them signed *Beilby pinxit*. Others, very closely related in style but unsigned, can only be attributed to the brush of William, but were very probably done by him. Perhaps the most striking examples of his work are the bucket-bowled goblets, each on an opaque white twist stem, the bowls painted with the Royal coat of

75

Fig. 37
Goblet painted in colours with the Royal
arms by William Beilby, perhaps to celebrate the birth of the Prince of Wales, later
George IV, in 1762. Height 9 inches.

arms of George II and George III (Fig. 37), of which a signed example is recorded. As each bears also the Prince of Wales's Feathers, it is probable that they were made to celebrate the birth of the future George IV, which took place in 1762.

The Beilby glasses were executed, so far as is known, between 1762 and 1778. In the latter year, Mrs. Beilby died and her son and daughter left Newcastle for Scotland. There, it has been suggested, they may have continued to paint glass, and certain pieces bearing Scottish subjects have been put forward in support of the idea. It is not, however, generally accepted, and the assumption is that William and his sister turned to another source of livelihood on crossing the Border.

Less rare than the preceding glasses, but often equally decorative and eagerly sought after, are those bearing on them emblems of the Jacobites. Mostly they were ornamented on the wheel, but a proportion was enamelled or diamond-engraved. They have been studied closely and continuously since the end of the last century, and more has been written about them than about any other type of English glass. Their fascination increases with their growing rarity, for although a few unrecorded examples come to light from year to year their supply diminishes through museum acquisitions and breakages. At the same time, more people become interested in the subject and swell the ranks of those who want to own a specimen.

The Jacobites were given their name because they believed in the cause of James (Jacobus) II and his descendants: members of the Royal house of Stuart. James became a convert to Roman Catholicism, and his second wife, Mary of Modena, shared with him that faith. He succeeded as King in 1685, but when his religious beliefs, and his actions in support of them, proved unpopular he fled to France. His place on the throne was taken by the Protestant William of Orange, husband of James II's sister. Another sister, Anne, succeeded William, but she died without leaving any living children. As a result, the throne passed to the great-grandson of James I, George, ruler (Elector) of Hanover, in Germany.

It is a somewhat complex genealogy, with race, religion and politics intermingled, so it cannot be wondered that people were divided in their allegiance. The situation was further aggravated by the fact that in 1688 Mary of Modena bore James a son, Prince James Francis Edward Stuart. The Jacobites considered him to be the true heir to the English throne and that he should reign in place of George I. They rallied to him both openly and in secret, and in due time he earned the sobriquet 'The Old Pretender'. The Prince lived in France, and made two attempts to land in

Fig. 38
Detail of wine-glass bowl on an air-twist stem, the former engraved with a profile portrait of the Young Pretender and Jacobite emblems.

Scotland where, in 1715, he stayed for a short time before returning hurriedly whence he had come. His marriage in 1719 was followed by the birth of a son, Prince Charles Edward, who was known as 'The Young Pretender'. The latter also attempted an invasion of the British Isles, and in 1745, having landed in the Hebrides, marched as far as Derby before being driven back and

Double (gemmel) flask in striped glass with trailed ornament on the sides and blue mouth rims. Nailsea type, early nineteenth century. Length 8¾ inches.

Wine bottle showing the 'kick' beneath the base. Early eighteenth century.

decisively beaten at Culloden. Both father and son did little to encourage the sympathy of their followers, both being unstable in their relationships with their wives, the younger adding drunkenness to his vices.

It seems probable that the majority of those who professed to be Jacobites were intrigued by the notion of belonging to a group of a secret or semi-secret nature, although probably very few of the

Fig. 39
Set of wine-glasses on air-twist stems, the bowl of each engraved with a Jacobite rose and the word 'Fiat' and the foot with oak leaves about 'Redi'. About 1750. Height 6¼ inches.

gatherings were wholeheartedly treasonable. Much of the activity centred in Wales and the north-west of England, where the 'Cycle Club', based on Wrexham, was prominent. In some instances there was confusion between Tories and Jacobites, so it is now uncertain whether some of the political coteries of the day did or did not combine the Stuart cause with their own.

Some of the clubs had distinctive emblems engraved on glasses and decanters employed for ceremonies commemorating 'The King over the Water' or 'The Steward of the Realm', the latter alluding to the Stuarts holding the office of Stewards of Scotland. Many other toasts, more or less ambiguous or treasonable, no doubt had their day and are long forgotten, only the glasses in which they were drunk now remaining.

The most important of them all are the 'Amen' glasses, of which fewer than a score are recorded. They are decorated with diamond-engraving, and the principal ornament is a treasonable distortion of the national anthem, 'God Save the King', in up to

Fig. 40
Decanter and steeple-shaped stopper, the body engraved with a rose spray and bud and pairs of barley ears. About 1750. Height about 9 inches.

as many as four verses. They date probably from about 1745, and have been reproduced in the present century.

The wheel-engraved glasses and decanters, which form the majority of existing specimens, bear one or more of a number of emblems which are associated with the Jacobite cause. Argument has prevailed about some of them, for it is not always clear, 200 years later, what some of the motifs signify, but the best-known of them are the following:

Rose: although it is certain that the White Rose was a Jacobite emblem, it has been disputed whether it applied to the Old

Pretender or to the House of Stuart as a whole. It was at one time considered that the Rose represented the Pretender and the buds were his two sons, but it is now thought that the flower stood for the English Crown and the buds for the two Pretenders, father and son.

Thistle: predictably represents the Crown of Scotland, and is found growing from the same stem as the Rose.

Star: alludes to the birth of the Young Pretender, but possibly it signifies the 'guiding light' of the Jacobite movement.

Other emblems associated with the cult are a bee, a cobweb, a butterfly and grub, an oak leaf and a compass. Their significance has been much debated, and the appearance of one or more of them on a glass is important in determining the rarity of a specimen. In addition to the floral and other motifs, glasses were often inscribed with legends in Latin, which included:

Fiat: May it happen.
Revirescit: He grows strong again.
Redi (or *Redite* or *Redeat*): May he return.
Reddas Incolumen: May you return safely.

Some surviving glasses bear portraits, most often of the Young Pretender, executed on the wheel but in a few instances in enamel. Often they are inscribed in Latin with legends such as *Audentior Ibo* (I will go more boldly, Fig. 41) or *Hic Vir Hic Est* (This, this is the man). Others, very few in number, show the head of Flora Macdonald, who assisted the escape of the Prince after the rout of the battle of Culloden.

The Jacobite glasses were current between about 1745 and 1765, and as they have been studied and collected for several decades there is now no shortage of forgeries. These are not only completely new glasses but also take the more deceptive form of genuinely old examples with modern engraving. An experienced eye is usually needed to distinguish the authentic from the fake.

Also used for the drinking of loyal toasts, but in the Protestant and loyal causes, were the Williamite glasses showing a portrait of King William III of Orange. The monarch is usually depicted on horseback, but sometimes only in head and shoulders, and his name often forms part of the inscription. The latter occasionally refers to the battle of the river Boyne, in which William's troops defeated those of James II in 1690.

Williamite glasses are rarer than those commemorating the

Fig. 41
Wine-glass, the bowl engraved with a portrait of the Young Pretender and on the
foot a thistle. About 1750. Height about
6½ inches.

Fig. 42
Wine-glass on an opaque twist stem, the
bowl engraved with a portrait of Flora
Macdonald, who aided the escape of
Prince Charles Edward (the Young
Pretender) after the Battle of Culloden.
About 1750. Height 5¾ inches.

Jacobites, and range in date from about 1740 to the last decades
of the century. It is argued that many, if not most, of the glasses
were engraved in Ireland, where a Dublin glass-house announced
in 1752 that it supplied engraving 'of any kind or pattern . . .
toasts or any flourish whatsoever'. Inscriptions range from the

Fig. 43
Wine-glass on an opaque twist stem, the
bowl inscribed GLORIOUS MEMORY
KING WILLIAM III BOYNE and dated
1690. About 1750. Height 6⅝ inches.

brief THE GLORIOUS MEMORY to the resounding and lengthy:

TO THE GLOREOUS PIOUS AND IMMORTAL MEMORY OF THE GREAT AND GOOD KING WILLIAM WIIO FREED US FROM POPE AND POPERY KNAVERY AND SLAVERY BRASS MONEY AND WOODEN SHOES. AND HE WHO REFUSES THIS TOAST MAY BE DAMNED CRAMMED AND RAMMED DOWN THE GREAT GUN OF ATHLONE.

This last, it may be added, appears on a goblet, 8 inches in height, in the Philadelphia Museum.

The foregoing are not the only causes of which reminders may be seen in the form of eighteenth-century wine-glasses. The adherents of John Wilkes toasted 'Wilkes and Liberty' as well as the notorious No. 45 of the journal *The North Briton* which got their hero into so much trouble. The taxing of cider in 1763 resulted in the making of special glasses for toasting the repeal of the duty. Coronations, election successes, freemasonry and family occasions were also commemorated by appropriate inscriptions and emblems.

The preceding pages have been devoted almost entirely to the various kinds of drinking-glasses made in the eighteenth century, but the material was used also for making many other articles. Some of them are now very scarce, some have survived but their original purpose is obsolete, and some have disappeared completely with no more than a mention in a newspaper to record their existence.

A few of the dealers of the time advertised their wares, and from such announcements an idea of what they sold can be gained. In 1752, Jerom Johnson, whose premises were in the Strand, London, informed the public in the following terms that he had in stock

> ...all sorts of fine Flint Glasses, brilliant Lustres, Branches, Candlesticks, Dishes, Plates, Bowls, Basons, Cups and Covers, Saucers, Saltcellars, cut Bottles, Decanters, Rummers ... Desart Glasses of all sorts ... Salvers ... cruets and Castors; curious Lamps, Wash-hand Glasses ... and finest polish'd Mugs, and Pitchers ... Wholesale and Retail, at the most reasonable Rates ...

Fig. 44
Candlestick with a Silesian stem. About
1720. Height 10½ inches.

Of the articles mentioned, those most likely to be seen nowadays include:

Candlesticks: Some surviving hollow-stemmed candlesticks date from the end of the seventeenth century. With the introduction of lead glass came sticks that are of similar pattern

Fig. 45
Candlestick cut all over with facets. About 1765. Height about 7 inches.

to those of brass and silver. Small-sized taper-sticks, for holding a taper to melt sealing-wax, similarly follow the style of metal ones.

Dishes, plates, cups and saucers: All of these have survived but only in small numbers. There were also glass plate-protectors, which were circular discs to fit in the well of a plate and save the delicately painted chinaware from being scratched during use.

Bowls: Some large-sized punch-bowls are recorded, and instead of being painted like china examples were engraved with scenes and inscriptions.

Saltcellars: These are occasionally seen, but silver doubtless proved more practical for the purpose.

Decanters: The ordinary wine-bottle would have looked out of place on a dining-table laden with polished silver and

87

Fig. 46
Decanters with engraved labels. About
1760. Height about 11 inches.

Fig. 47
Decanters with cut and engraved decoration. 1760–70. Heights about $9\frac{1}{2}$ to 11 inches.

shining chinaware, so the wine was poured into containers made for the purpose. Late seventeenth-century decanters or wine-jugs had a handle and a loose-fitting stopper. The more familiar type, with a ground-in stopper to keep the contents airtight, began to appear in about the early 1750s. Some had the name of a wine engraved or painted on the front, but this was largely discontinued when bottle-tickets (wine-labels) became popular in about 1760. The shapes of decanters, as well as their ornamentation, varied from time to time in conformity with fashion.

Rummers: The roemer was a round-bowled drinking-glass with a broad hollow foot, usually with a series of circular seals (prunts) round the fat stem. George Ravenscroft made them in imitation of foreign examples, but their use died out early in the eighteenth century. Rummers are large-bowled glasses usually raised on squat feet, the latter being round or square according to fashion.

89

Dessert glasses: Custards, jellies and other desserts were served in short glasses with one or two handles, often set in the centre of the table on a glass salver: the latter of a circular shape with a hollow foot. Two or three of the laden salvers would be stood one on top of another, to form a pyramid as a centre-piece.

Castors: For sugar, pepper and other powdered condiments.

Wash-hand glasses: A term for finger-bowls, which were used regularly at the table from about 1750 onwards.

Last, but by no means of the least importance, are what Johnson lists as 'Lustres' and 'Branches', meaning what we know now as candelabra and chandeliers. The latter had been made of glass from at least 1714, when an advertiser announced that he had for sale 'Glass Schandeliers'. Earlier, they were composed of metal hung with polished rock-crystal, and no doubt it was inevitable that English lead glass should be employed successfully for the

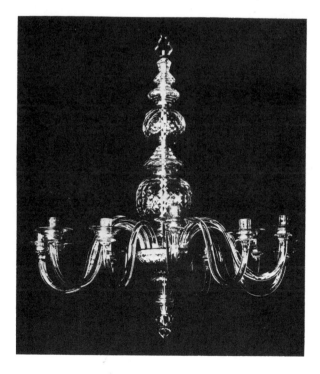

Fig. 48
Twelve-light chandelier formerly at Thornham Hall, Suffolk. About 1735. Height about 4 feet.

90

Fig. 49
Chandelier ornamented with cutting and
hung with round and pear-shaped drops.
About 1780.

same purpose. In fact, not only was it shaped and cut into the pendent drops, but it was fashioned into the central stem and curved arms which were arranged to conceal a metal interior framework.

Although suspended high up in a room where it might be thought their long-term preservation would be assured, changes of fashion affected them as well as everything else. Styles of cutting, shallow at first and then deep, the curvature of the arms and the form of the stem all changed from time to time, and led to one

91

style of chandelier after another being discarded. None older than about 1730–40 has survived.

Until about 1780 the chandelier was given a number of arms springing from the stem, and while at first they supported a few score of drops they were later 'connected' by long strings of them. By the end of the century, the strings had increased in quantity

Fig. 50
Chandelier, the gilt metal frame hung with strings of cut drops and with 'icicles'. About 1815.

so that the stem was concealed by them and they formed a kind of bag (Fig. 50).

Candelabra were commonly made for two lights, although a three-light example, attributed to about 1695, is in the Victoria and Albert Museum. The majority of extant examples date from about 1770, when they were made in pairs to stand on tables in front of mirrors. Their designs vary, but always incorporate a maximum of cutting to reflect the candle flames. Some are completely of glass, but others include gilt metal, painted and gilt glass (Fig. 52), and Wedgwood jasperware.

92

Fig. 51
Candelabrum, cut and hung with drops.
About 1790.

Fig. 52
Candlestick with cut-glass nozzle and grease-pan, the base of white glass decorated in gold and the whole mounted in gilt metal. About 1790. Height about 7 inches.

In addition to the wares advertised by Johnson, mention may be made of two others ·

Cream or milk jugs: These, like china ones, follow the shapes of silver jugs. Glass examples are now scarce.

Sweetmeats: Glass stands for holding small quantities of sweetmeats at the table were made from the late seventeenth century onwards. They are in appearance like a modern champagne glass, with a broad flat bowl and a stem and foot similar to an ordinary wine-glass. Some have shaped and ornamented rims which would make them impossible to drink from, but the plainer types are sometimes referred to as champagnes.

All the foregoing were made in London and at the numerous glass-houses dotted about the country. On the whole it is

94

Pair of candlesticks with cut ornament and hanging cut drops. About 1820. Height 6½ inches.

Blue glass tankard inscribed in gold 'Friendship'. Bristol type, early nineteenth century. Height 4¾ inches.

impossible to distinguish pieces made in the provinces from those of the capital: both used similar metal and both slavishly followed fashion so that the appearance of one piece or another is very similar. Two of the provincial centres did, however, make wares with distinctive features: King's Lynn and Newcastle upon Tyne.

King's Lynn, in the north-west of Norfolk, is the site of sand suitable for glass-making, and by the end of the seventeenth

Fig. 53
(*Top row*) Pair of salts, pair of stands, perhaps for sweetmeats, and a two-handled cup; (*bottom row*) five glasses for sweetmeats, the outer two with Silesian stems. First half of the eighteenth century.

century a glass-works had been opened there. In 1693 the owners were two men, Francis Jackson and John Straw, who also had premises in London. Jackson stated two years later that he had given up the Norfolk establishment, and there is no further record of its existence until 1747. In that year the *Ipswich Journal* printed an advertisement stating:

To be sold by the glass-house in Lynn, a large quantity of fine Flint-Glass both figured and plain, well sorted, the stock consisting of a great Variety of the most Valuable

95

sorts of drinking Glasses, Decanters, Salvers and other glassware.

Dating from about 1760 are a number of glasses and decanters which are attributed to the manufactory. All show the same peculiarity: the body is marked by a series of horizontal ribs, shallow but clearly discernible (Fig. 54). The attribution was made in 1897 by Albert Hartshorne, who gave no reason for it. A later writer repeated it, adding that he knew of two glasses of the type that had been purchased in the area, so that 'the conjecture may reasonably be accepted'.

Fig. 54
Tumbler of King's Lynn type with a horizontally ribbed body. About 1760. Height 4⅞ inches.

Newcastle upon Tyne boasted a number of glass-works from the mid-seventeenth century, when the first was started there by a family named Dagnia. During the eighteenth century the drinking glasses made in the city can often be recognised by their light and graceful baluster stems, which often enclose elaborate air-twists. The lead metal has a brilliant surface, and some of the Newcastle glasses are among the most attractive made.

They were exported to both Scandinavia and Holland, and in the latter country were often selected for embellishment by Dutch engravers. Ornament was applied by the wheel and also by diamond-point; the exquisite work in the latter medium by Wolff, Greenwood and others is frequently found to have been

96

Fig. 55
Pair of Newcastle wine-glasses with air-twist stems, the bowls engraved with fruiting vine and butterflies. About 1760. Height about 8½ inches.

executed on Newcastle glasses. At home, many Jacobite commemorative glasses are of Newcastle type and, not unexpectedly, William and Mary Beilby used them for their enamel-painting.

Finally, there were the glass-houses in and about Bristol, to which much is allocated but little can be proved authentic. When Houghton made his list (page 61) there were nine glass-houses in operation, and in the course of the eighteenth century the

Fig. 56
Bristol blue glass: two sets of spirit decanters with gilt labels, and four sauce bottles similarly labelled and each cut with a band of diamonds round the shoulder. Late eighteenth century. Average height of spirit decanters 10 inches.

number was increased. While clear lead glass was made there, it is the coloured that has its name inseparably linked with the city.

Green, amethyst and, particularly, deep blue are the colours attributed almost automatically to one or other of the Bristol makers, although there is no doubt that they were also made elsewhere. That a proportion came from Bristol is undoubtedly true, and a number of blue decanters, finger bowls and dishes that were made there have been preserved. On the underside of each is pencilled in gold: I. Jacobs Bristol. It is the mark of Isaac Jacobs,

Fig. 57
Bristol blue glass finger-bowl stand decorated in gilt with a band of Greek Key pattern and a crest. Signed by Isaac Jacobs. About 1810. Diameter $7\frac{3}{4}$ inches.

Fig. 58
Gilt mark of Isaac Jacobs, the Non-such Flint Glass Manufactory, Bristol, about 1805–35.

99

who continued to run a business started by his father Lazarus Jacobs (died 1796), and was appointed Glass-maker to George III.

Opaque white glass has been mentioned earlier as a component of the twist stems of wine-glasses, but the same material was used on its own to make articles closely simulating porcelain. Some was manufactured at Bristol, which was once thought to have been the sole English source of supply, but it was made also

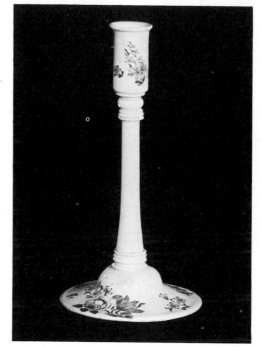

Fig. 59
Candlestick of opaque white glass enamelled in colours. About 1760. Height 9 inches.

in the Midlands and the North-west. Vases, candlesticks and other pieces were painted in the same manner as chinaware, and the name of a Bristol resident, Michael Edkins, is associated with much of the work.

Because a business ledger that belonged to Edkins has been preserved (in the City Art Gallery, Bristol), some details of his career are known. He painted pottery as well as glass, and also gilded blue glass. At one time most of the surviving decorated opaque white glass (known in the past as *enamel*) was attributed

100

Fig. 60
Opaque white glass vase enamelled in
colours with a Chinese scene in imitation
of porcelain. About 1760. Height about 7
inches.

to the brush of Edkins, but the work is now thought with good reason to have been executed in Staffordshire on articles made in that area.

A few miles outside Bristol, at Nailsea, a glass-house was started towards the end of the eighteenth century. All kinds of trifles are popularly stated to have been made there, although it is a fact that such objects were made also in numerous other places and long after the close of the century. Nonetheless, as with coloured Bristol ware, it is convenient to give a name to things, and once one has been acquired it usually persists in spite of its having been discredited.

A twentieth-century glass-maker, Harry J. Powell, wrote about Nailsea and its products in a book published in 1923 and said:

The great Nailsea works were famous for the fine quality of their crown window-glass, but are unworthily commemorated in museums and private collections by the rude vases,

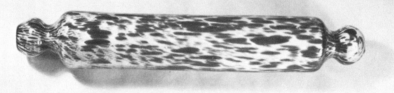

Fig. 61
Rolling pin of white glass splashed with red and blue. Nailsea type. Early nineteenth century. Length 14 inches.

flasks, jugs, candlesticks and rolling-pins originally made by the glass-blowers in their spare time. They are colourless or coloured, and many are marked, spotted, streaked or roughly threaded with opaque white enamel or crude-coloured glasses. Similar objects known colloquially as 'friggers' may be seen as chimney-piece ornaments in glass-blowers' homes in every glass-making district. In the Bristol district these by-products were exploited by dealers and became for a time staple products. They were widely distributed, and copies are still made in many districts and sold as antiques. Even the originals, with very few exceptions, are entirely devoid of artistic, technical or historic interest.

Not everyone will agree with Powell's assessment of friggers as being 'entirely devoid of artistic, technical or historic interest'.

102

In spite of that statement, or perhaps in ignorance of it, very many people buy and collect Nailsea ware. To the list given can be added walking-sticks, 'yards of ale', model sailing-vessels, miniature representations of hunts with the hounds in full cry, hats, pipes and hand-bells. Many of them are much later in date than may be thought, for their manufacture continued throughout the nineteenth century and later and most existing specimens, if at all old, are Victorian.

As regards modern copies of such articles, the position today differs little from the time when Powell was writing. Twentieth-century 'genuine antique' friggers are still being made, and much coloured 'Bristol' glass mistakenly accepted as authentic and old was made far, far away in Czechoslovakia.

6. The Nineteenth Century

By the year 1800 the duty on glass, which had been imposed in 1745, had risen from 9s. 4d. to 21s. 5½d. per hundredweight (112 lb.). In spite of this burden, the industry flourished, and the tax on weight would seem to have had little or no effect on the style of articles that were made. Paradoxically, almost all glassware was massive in comparison with that made a hundred years earlier, and few surfaces were left plain that could be decorated with cutting. As the century progressed, the use of the wheel increased, patterns grew more and more complex and the natural appearance of the material was replaced by a dazzling glitter.

Despite the daunting intricacy of the designs and the difficult nature of the material, the craftsmen produced work with a mechanical precision of finish. The more exotic examples of their skilful handiwork bristle with jagged and pointed ornament, so that to handle them ungloved might invite laceration. Nonetheless, the results were admired universally and copied by glassmakers in France, Bohemia and elsewhere, and English cut glass (or 'cut crystal', as it is sometimes called) gained a position it still enjoys.

The introduction of steam-driven cutting machinery undoubtedly assisted the workers, who thenceforward need no longer rely on slower and hesitant treadle-operated wheels. The change took place from about 1810, but there were doubtless plenty of

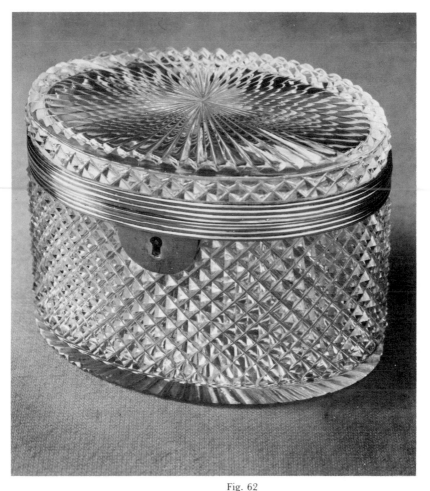

Fig. 62
Oval box, the hinged lid cut with radiating flutes and the body with diamonds. About 1820. Height about 4 inches.

workshops that continued to employ foot-power. After all, even if it was slower it was also cheaper, and considerable capital expense was involved in the installation of a steam-engine. Only trial and error would convince the more conservative-minded

Fig. 63
Pair of candlesticks with stepped bases and cut shades. About 1830. Height about 13 inches.

Fig. 64
Two-light candelabrum with gilt metal arms, the base step-cut, the nozzles cut with diamonds and the whole hung with 'icicles'. About 1820. Height 19½ inches.

makers, and once they had changed to power they soon discovered
that increased output recouped them.

However cheaply cut glassware could be made with the aid of
steam-power, its cost remained too high for the mass of the people

Fig. 65
Decanters with mushroom-shaped
stoppers. First quarter of nineteenth
century. Average height 10 inches.

who wanted to buy it. Their wants were supplied by imitation cutting produced in moulds; the articles were blown into patterned moulds constructed to hinge open and release the finished articles. Fire-polishing gave a bright finish, removed general roughness and more or less eradicated signs of where the mould joined.

While quite a large amount of the treadle- and power-cut ware has survived, the blown-moulded has largely vanished. Cheap to

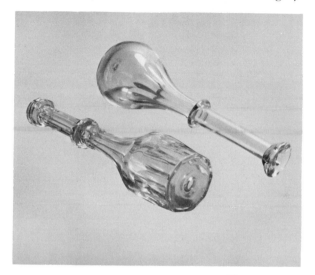

Fig. 66
Two toddy-lifters for serving punch. The bulbous end was placed in the liquid, a thumb or finger put over the top, the lifter withdrawn and held over a glass, and on freeing the hole at the top the punch was released. About 1830. Length 6¾ inches.

buy, it had plenty of daily use and inevitably got smashed. Mould-blown decanters are not especially scarce, but are difficult to date with any accuracy. The moulds were expensive to make, so were kept in use over many years.

The year 1845 was an important one in the history of the English glass industry, for it marked the end of the duty which had been laid on it for a complete century. The last years of the tax were particularly burdensome, because it was levied on the batch and not just on the product. The contents of the pot, everything comprising the metal, cullet as well, was weighed and charged for. Long afterwards, Harry J. Powell recollected what he had seen of

Fig. 67
Goblet engraved with a representation of
Nelson's funeral car and made in com-
memoration of his burial in 1805. Height
5⅛ inches.

Fig. 68
Goblet engraved with an urn on a tomb-
stone and inscribed QUEEN CAROLINE
DIED AUGT. 7 1821. Height 4⅞ inches.

110

Pair of green glass decanters and stoppers with gilt decoration. About 1845. Height 14 inches.

Sweetmeat basket of white, blue and clear glass, the interior inset with spangles. Late nineteenth century. Height 7 inches.

Fig. 69
Goblet engraved with ears of barley, fruiting vine and flowers, and dated September 1837. Height 7¾ inches.

traces remaining from the tax-gatherers at the old Whitefriars Glassworks, in London:

The sites only remain of the sentry-boxes in which the 'officers of excise' spent such part of their time in sleep as was not occupied in harrying the works' managers or being harried by the glass-house boys. Two, at least, of these officers were quartered in every glass-works, and as the duty was payable partly on the worked and partly on the unworked glass, it was their business to register the total weight of

111

glass and to prevent the removal of any piece of manufactured glass which had not been weighed.

Giving evidence before the Commissioners of Excise in 1833, a manufacturer spoke with great bitterness of his experience and he doubtless voiced the feelings of most of his fellows:

Our business and premises are placed under the arbitrary control of a class of men to whose will and caprice it is most irksome to have to submit and this under a system of regulations most ungraciously inquisitorial. We cannot enter into parts of our own premises without their permission; we can do no one single act in the conduct of our business without having previously notified our intention to the officers placed over us. We have in the course of the week's operations to serve some sixty or seventy notices on these, our masters, and this under heavy penalties of from £200 to £500 for every separate neglect.

Small wonder, therefore, that illicit glass-houses flourished, and it was reported that some £65,000 of goods on which duty had not been paid was sold annually in London alone. What the figure was for the whole country is not known, but there must have been innumerable back-street kilns making rough-and-ready articles for quick and cheap sale.

The middle years of the century are very well documented owing to the enormous amount of activity in connexion with the Great Exhibition. This was held in Hyde Park, London, between 1st May and 11 October 1851 and visited by 6,039,195 people. The total of 100,000 or so exhibits was housed in a vast iron-framed building, resembling a conservatory, fitted with more than 293,000 panes of glass, which caused the magazine *Punch* to dub it the 'Crystal Palace'.

The official four-volume *Catalogue* of the Exhibition contains details of all the exhibits, and woodcut illustrations of some of them. In addition, there were numerous other publications in which the more interesting items on display were discussed and, again, many of them were pictured. There is no lack of information about the glassware available to the public in that year, although it must be remembered that a proportion of it was doubtless specially made for the purpose. An international exhibition invariably calls forth minor masterpieces of technical skill that are not always representative of their kind.

In the last category was the fountain, 27 feet high, which stood in a principal intersection in the building. It was composed of no less than four tons of glass, with the principal dish having a diameter of 8 feet and the water falling in three separate masses (Fig. 70). The makers, Osler's of Birmingham, also showed a pair

Fig. 70
Osler's glass fountain at the Great Exhibition, 1851. A contemporary woodcut.

113

of 8-foot-tall candelabra, each for fifteen lights, which had been a birthday present to the Queen from her husband, Prince Albert, in 1849.

The fountain, placed so conspicuously, was greatly admired, but although it was recommended for the award of a medal it did not receive one. In view of the popular misconception that the Victorians liked nothing more than sheer size and glitter, it may be of interest to reprint some remarks made about the piece at the time. They were written by Richard Redgrave, a painter who later became art director of the South Kensington (later Victoria and Albert) Museum and also surveyor of the Royal pictures.

Redgrave wrote a very lengthy report on the design of objects at the Exhibition, and in the course of it commented on the glass fountain in the following words:

It is a matter of regret that a production so unique in this material should not be entitled to praise for its design; the truth is, that works of the like magnitude in glass never having been before attempted, and the designer being consequently thrown on his own resources, he should have seized the opportunity so offered, and, striving to forget what had been done in other departments, treated the material for itself alone, and consistently with its own proper requirements. Instead of this there is an attempt to mix architectural stone forms with others that have become almost conventional in glass, and the result is inconsistent and unsatisfactory. The glass pillars are far too slight for the heavy inverted canopy, and both those canopies are too large for the basins above, very inharmonious in their contrast of lines, and unfitted for the agreeable display of the water; . . . indeed it is evident that the main source of error has been in supposing glass, and especially cut glass, a suitable material for a fountain; it is at once seen that this is not the case; instead of its being a proper foil for the sparkling water, glass emulates its sparkle and lustre, and the result is a failure from want of contrast.

Undoubtedly an international exhibition would call forth all kinds of incongruities of this nature; misuses contrived deliberately for advertising purposes, but which would not be intended to be taken seriously. None the less, the age was one in which such misuses were not confined to any one material or solely to public display—many articles for the home were as inappro-

114

priate in their design as the strongly condemned fountain. However, indiscretions of this nature are more obvious in retrospect, and they were largely unnoticed at the time.

Typical of the exhibits in 1851 of several other Birmingham firms was that of George Bacchus and Sons (Fig. 71), which was entered in the catalogue as follows:

Flower-stand, with vase and cornucopias. Vase, cased enamel on ruby, engraved. Grape dish. Decanter, threaded and engraved. Tazza, with spiral stem. Groups of wine glasses,

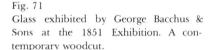

Fig. 71
Glass exhibited by George Bacchus & Sons at the 1851 Exhibition. A contemporary woodcut.

champagne glasses, and goblets. Sugar-basin and butter-dish, cased, enamel on green, with gold leafage.

Decanters, flint glass, cut and engraved. Goblets, various colours, cut and ornamented. Claret jug. Card-dish, cased, blue, on flint, cut in diamond panels, &c. Vase, cased, ruby and white, cut and ornamented; vase, cased, enamel on flint, cut and engraved.

Jug, cased, enamel on blue flint, cut, engraved, and gilt, with goblet. Jug, cornelian, with goblet. Decanter, Pomona green, cut. Champagne decanter, cased, ruby on flint, cut and engraved, with champagne glass. Cut-glass vase, 'cased'. Wine, claret, and champagne glasses, cased, coloured, and flint glass, cut, engraved, &c. Cut-glass butter-dish, cased, enamel on yellow. Vase, green and white, ornamented. Cut-glass centre dish and stand, green.

Similarly, Davis, Greathead & Green, of Stourbridge, showed amongst much else

A great variety of vases, jars, and scent-jars, and scent-jars for holding flowers, &c., in the Egyptian, Etruscan, and Grecian styles; many of them cut, coated, gilt, painted in enamel colours, after the antique, with figures, ornaments, flowers, landscapes, and marine views, of the following colours, viz., ruby, oriental blue, chrysoprase, turquoise, black, rose colour, opal-coated blue, cornelian, opal frosted, pearl opal, mazareen blue, &c.
The whole of the labour and ornamentation performed by English workmen.

Those two firms alone showed a large variety of goods, both as regards the different articles and the many styles in which each was made. The range of colours is a striking feature, with clear flint taking a back position and such eye-catchers as chrysoprase (apple green) and ruby to the forefront. A high degree of skill was expended in such techniques as casing and cutting, and the decorative inspirations ranged from ancient Egypt and Greece to Venice and the France of Francis I.

Other exhibitors showed comparable articles and one firm, Rice Harris and Son, Islington Glass Works, Birmingham, had 'pressed and moulded glass tumblers, goblets, wines, sugar-basins, butter-coolers, salt-cellars, honey-pots, door knobs &c.' The press-and-mould process had been evolved in the United States in the late 1820s, and was introduced in England a few years later. Although articles made by it appeared at the 1851 Exhibition, their manufacture did not take place on a large scale for a further decade or two. However, sufficient was being made in the mid-century to start something of a revulsion against cut-glass, which pressing imitated closely and occasionally deceptively.

In his book *The Stones of Venice,* published in 1853, John Ruskin, whose pronouncements on all aspects of art were almost final at the time, gave his considered views on the subject. Not only did he roundly condemn all cutting, but gave as his reason the insubstantial nature of the material which rendered it pointless to expend much labour on anything so breakable.

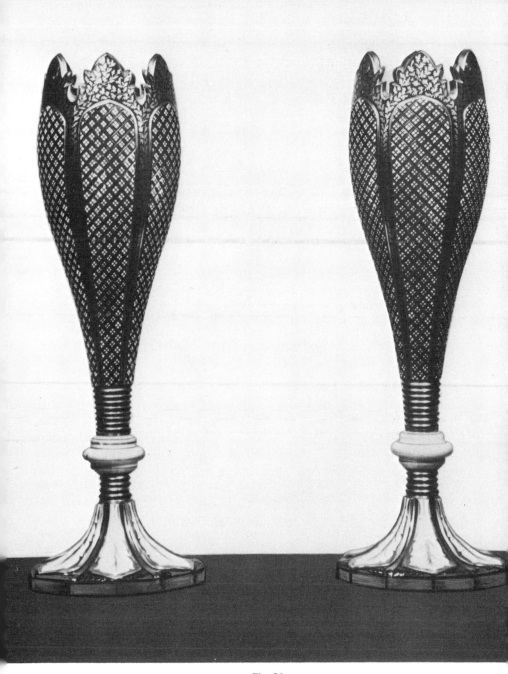

Fig. 72
Pair of vases of ruby glass cased in white
and decorated with cutting and gilding.
About 1850. Height about 12 inches.

Ruskin's words, in part, are:

> ... all cut glass is barbarous ... Also, all very neat, finished, and perfect form in glass is barbarous: for this fails in proclaiming another of its great virtues; namely, the ease with which its light substance can be moulded or blown into any form, so long as perfect accuracy be not required ...

He then suggested how glass should be treated, and continued:

> ... no delicate outlines are to be attempted, but only such fantastic and fickle grace as the mind of the workman can conceive and execute on the instant. The more wild, extravagant, and grotesque in their gracefulness the forms are, the better ... while we triumphantly set forth its transparency, we are also frankly to admit its fragility, and therefore not to waste much time upon it, nor put any real art into it when intended for daily use.

Finally, in a single sentence, he summed up his views, which favoured a return of the intuitive blower and manipulator in place of the painstakingly laborious work of the cutter. Ruskin's words are:

> No workmen ought ever to spend more than an hour in the making of any glass vessel.

At the time he wrote the majority of the glass on the market was, like most other decorative objects, overladen with ornament. It is no wonder Ruskin protested, for cutting was applied for the sheer pleasure of exploiting new shapes and skills, and without considering properly whether they were really suitable for glass. Whether, in fact, they brought out the best qualities of the substance—the 'inner fire'—or whether they just made it hideous and more costly. Ruskin's words may, in the light of present taste, be seen to be applied fairly with regard to cut-glass of the 1850s, but it is incorrect to think that late eighteenth/early nineteenth century work deserves the same sweeping condemnation.

Less noticed at the time than cut-glass, probably because it was little more than a passing fashion and was sold inexpensively, was glass with a matt finish. The French had made a speciality of opaline glass (*verre opaline*) since early in the the century, but this was a material with a milky appearance that only seemed dull and actually had a normal shining finish. A similar glassware was made in England, and this matt one may have been produced as a

118

Fig. 73
Pair of opal glass vases decorated with bands of flowers in colours and gilt. About 1850. Height about 24 inches.

cheap or alternative version of it. All kinds of objects were given a dull, unglasslike finish, ranging from plates and dishes to portrait busts of celebrities.

F. & C. Osler, who displayed the large fountain at the Great Exhibition, made what are listed in the catalogue as:

Busts of Shakespeare, Milton, Scott, and Peel, in frosted glass.

119

Fig. 74
Set of three opal glass vases painted in colours with bunches of flowers. About 1850.

Fig. 75
Grape-dish of matt white glass, marked PATENTED AUG 31 1875. Probably made by John Ford, Edinburgh. Length 7¾ inches.

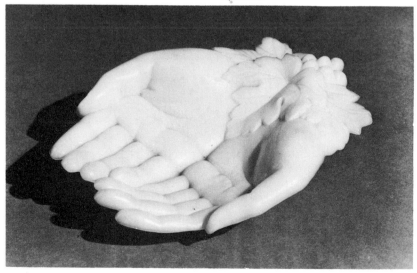

Beneath the brief entry is a note signed with the initials W. C. A., which reads :

These busts are produced in moulds, and the enamel or bright surface of the glass is removed by abrasion or grinding ; their effect is pleasant, and would seem to indicate that larger works might with propriety be under-taken of the same kind of material.

Matt-surfaced glass continued to be made for some decades and by several firms, but the advice of W. C. A. does not seem to have been heeded. Large works in the material do not seem to have been attempted, and his suggestion that it would 'afford a medium for the production of statues and monumental erections superior to marble' was, happily, ignored or, if tried, proved unsuccessful.

Both the Birmingham firms of Bacchus & Sons and Rice Harris & Son, and the Whitefriars Glassworks, London, are known to have made versions of the coloured glass paperweights which were a distinctive product of the French factories of Baccarat, Clichy and St Louis—the latter, in turn, having been inspired by those made by Bigaglia of Murano and in Bohemia. The English ones show different combinations of paler colours and lack the assured finish of the French. They were being produced in London and Birmingham by 1849, but as they are not mentioned in the 1851 Exhibition *Catalogue* it is possible that visitors there were denied a sight of them. Their production was not on a large scale, and the Whitefriars firm (now at Wealdstone, Middlesex) is the only one of the three to have remained in business and to have continued sporadically producing paperweights (Plate 16).

It is apposite to mention here the paperweights or doorstops of a green glass enclosing roughly moulded sulphides or air-bubbles. The latter were arranged either in some kind of pattern or were caused to resemble, often only vaguely, a pot of flowers (Fig. 76). Many of them were made by the firm of Kilner, of Wakefield, Yorkshire, and some bear seals like those found on wine-bottles (see Chapter 7) over the pontil-mark. They date from about 1830 onwards, but very few of them are anything like as old as that. All were the work of firms normally making bottles, hence the coloured glass, and as they were usually made from the glass left in the pot at the end of the day, which would otherwise have been thrown away or 'dumped', they acquired the name locally of *dumps*.

Many thousands of the visitors to the Crystal Palace must have

121

Fig. 76
Door stops or paperweights of pale green
glass, sometimes known as 'Dumps'.
Nineteenth century. Height 4¾ inches.

seen for the first time the enormous variety of effects that
could be achieved with glass, as well as the practical and im-
practical forms in which it would be produced. They must have returned to their homes eager to possess examples, and were ready
customers for any manufacturer who would make for them
suitable goods at a price they could afford to pay.

The answer lay in press-moulding, by which large amounts of
acceptable ware, superficially like the admired cut-glass, could be
made very cheaply. The simple process demanded that a lump
of molten metal was dropped into the heated mould, the plunger
squeezed the glass to take its shape and when the plunger was
withdrawn the article was more or less complete.

Finishing required a boy to pick up the article on an iron rod by
means of a dab of hot glass on its end, and then twirl it in the
glory-hole to give it a superficial shine by partially re-melting it.
This smoothed away any roughness, and remaining uneven edges
were quickly cut and pressed into shape by tools. It takes longer to
describe than to carry out, and it was recorded in 1858 that a good

122

team of 'five hands would produce a beautiful tumbler in about forty-five seconds'.

Articles made in this manner would have a mark beneath the base where the pontil was temporarily stuck on, but when the spring-loaded grip was employed it left no trace of its use. Unlike a mould-blown piece, the interior of a press-moulded one

Fig. 77
Pen tray and stand (in two separate parts) in the form of a boat, press-moulded in amber-coloured glass. Late nineteenth century. Length 10½ inches.

is smooth and does not follow within the patterning of the exterior. Tall items, such as vases and tumblers, were often unsatisfactory and emerged from the mould with an ugly crack running round the top about a quarter to half an inch below the rim. It was caused by the rapid cooling of the lump of glass in the mould prior to the lowering of the plunger, and when the latter descended the metal had begun to lose its ductility. After a time, the defect was eradicated.

There were three important makers of this cheap ware, and all were situated in the north-east of England. They were:

Sowerby's Ellison Glass Works, Gateshead-on-Tyne; Henry Greener & Co., Wear Glass Works, Sunderland; George Davidson & Co., Teams Glass Works, Gateshead-on-Tyne.

All three had an individual mark which was used on a proportion of their goods, and is to be found under the base, slightly raised on the surface like the impression of a seal (Fig. 78). The average size of each is about three-eighths of an inch high. Other makers used marks of a similar type, but as they were in a smaller way

Fig. 78
Marks found on press-moulded glass:
(*left to right*) Sowerby's Ellison Glass Works, Gateshead; Henry Greener & Co., Sunderland; George Davidson & Co., Gateshead.

of business examples of their productions are less often seen than those of the firms noted above.

In addition to a maker's mark, pieces also sometimes bear the diamond-shaped registration mark of the London Patent Office. This indicates that the design of the item bearing it was protected against copying for a period of three years following registry. The diamond mark has letters and numerals in the corners, and these indicate the name of the manufacturer, date and other details. Some of these can be deciphered with the aid of modern books of china marks, as the same signs were used on pottery and porcelain.

A report in the *Newcastle Daily Chronicle* in 1882 noted that Sowerby's was then the largest pressed glass manufactory in the world, and continued:

They cover an area of five and a half acres of ground, and from 700 to 1,000 hands are employed in them. . . . The production of the present time is about 150 tons per week of finished manufactured glass goods, and the materials necessary to make such an immense quantity of the substance may be said to be brought to Gateshead from the ends of the earth. . . . The factory works continually day and night, all the year round; the hands employed being divided into three shifts of eight hours each. One hour of each shift may be deducted for meals, so that the workpeople labour for no more than seven hours per diem. The staple articles of production are drinking glasses of various kinds, decanters, salt cellars, cake and fruit dishes and plates, with various objects in opaque glass. To the production of these goods in the manufactory there is practically no limit but the demand, and the rate at which they can be turned out of hand may be guessed from the fact that each man working at the moulds can make from 1,100 to 1,200 tumblers during his seven hours work. In the melting room are nine furnaces containing in all 78 pots more or less constantly in use. Each pot holds from twelve to fifteen hundredweight of molten glass.

The output of the ware was as varied in colour as it was enormous in quantity: clear and coloured, transparent and opaque, opal-like and, not least, the unusual *slag* glass. This last was a streaky material resembling marble, the name by which it is known in the United States, that included among its constituents a proportion of the waste slag from iron furnaces. Allegedly, the same ingredient had been one of the components of 'Ironstone China': a type of pottery introduced in Staffordshire in 1813. It is not clear whether the public connected the one with the other because of this common factor, but it is not improbable that because the one was so successful and durable it was considered that the other would be no less long-lasting.

Slag glass, usually in a deep purple or a dark turquoise, reached its height of popularity in the decades 1870-90, and it should be noted by potential buyers that it is still being made. At least one firm, Davidson's, are producing it and theirs can be deceptive because the modern articles continue to bear the same lion mark (Fig. 78) as the old. A glittering surface and an absence of wear-and-tear will betray a new piece, but both these indications can be made less obvious with the use of abrasives.

The majority of the articles were of small size, and took the form of spill-vases, 'tidies' and other containers. Basket-weave patterns were popular, and relief designs of the 1880s often show signs of the Japanese inspiration then current. Travelling bags, coal trucks, and boots and shoes were among the numerous homely models imitated in miniature, and carried out in garish colours, white or in a jet-black that hardly resembled glass at all.

The reaction against heavily cut ornament on more expensive

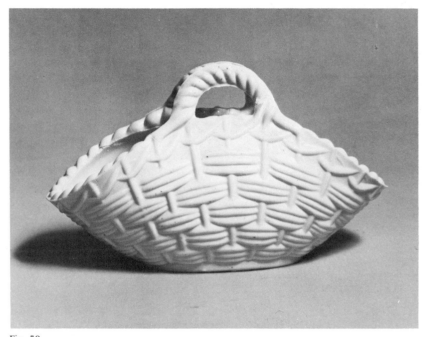

Fig. 79
Container of pale blue glass in the form of a basket, with Sowerby's peacock-head mark on the base. About 1880. Width 5 inches.

ware actually began a few years before Ruskin spoke out, when Henry Cole, soon to become one of the principal organisers of the Great Exhibition, started a venture named Summerly's Art Manufactures. Cole's scheme was to select what he considered were well-designed articles in pottery, metal, glass or other materials, and persuade manufacturers to produce them. They were marketed under his firm's name and for his activities in promoting sales he was paid a royalty.

Oil lamp and heater with ruby (cranberry) glass shade. Late nineteenth century. Overall height 19½ inches.

Ink bottle with millefiore decoration in base and stopper. Late nineteenth/early twentieth century. Height 3¾ inches.

One of the Summerly ventures was a set of drinking-glasses and a carafe, named the 'Well Spring', designed by Richard Redgrave and made by J. F. Christy, a Lambeth glass-maker, in 1847. The carafe, of which there is an example in the Victoria and Albert Museum, is of a simple inverted baluster form with a tall neck and curled flat mouth. The enamelled decoration is of green leaves, with a band of flower-heads encircling the neck. As the articles were intended for use with drinking-water, it was con-

Fig. 80
Pair of containers in the shape of shoes.
About 1880. Length about 4 inches.

sidered at the time highly appropriate that they should be decorated with water-plants.

Cole, however, tired of his scheme after a few years, either because it ceased to pay sufficiently well or because he was too busy with other ventures. In 1849, after a brief life of a couple of years, Summerly's Art Manufactures was terminated, and Cole turned his attention to the Great Exhibition. Working closely with the Prince

Consort, he was responsible for much of its enormous success and his eventual reward of a knighthood was fully earned.

It was notable at the 1851 exhibition that so much of the glassware was coloured, and much again was cased and cut as well as painted and gilded. Examples of this type of work had been produced in Bohemia from the early years of the century, and increasing quantities had been exported to England. Labouring under heavy taxation the foreign competition could not be met effectively, but after the tax was lifted in 1845 the position was different and strenuous attempts began to be made to rival the imported goods.

At the same time, impetus was given to the industry by the work in England of Georges Bontemps, a French glass-maker with a well-earned reputation on both sides of the Channel. At first he only acted as an adviser to Chance's, the Birmingham sheet-glass makers, but from 1848 took charge of their colour department. His researches into colouring stimulated others to do the same, and it is acknowledged that Bontemps had a considerable influence in this direction.

Clear glass articles were given a coating of colour with sometimes a layer of opaque white between the two, careful cutting removed unwanted coloured portions and left a series of shaped windows with neat white borders. Gilding and painting were sometimes added, and the finished pieces differed little from the garish porcelain popular at the time. A similar resemblance to chinaware is to be seen in the coloured and white opaline vases, which were often painted with great skill.

Cheaper versions of opaline were decorated by means of transfer prints touched-in with colour by hand, in the same manner as much pottery. The work was baked to make it permanent, and the effect, although very seldom comparable to hand workmanship, pleased the less discriminating public. An approximation to coloured glass was achieved by means of chemicals applied to the surface of clear objects, and the stain was likewise fired. The process was very much less expensive than using solid-coloured metal, but the range of tints was mostly confined to a deep ruby red and a brownish yellow. Stained pieces were usually given engraved ornament, when the excessively thin external colour is immediately apparent to a sharp eye.

The English coloured glass closely followed Bohemian prototypes, and today it is often impossible to distinguish the one from the other. Shapes, colours, styles of decoration and tech-

128

Fig. 81
Mantelpiece ornament or lustre, of ruby glass overlaid with white, painted and gilt, and hung with cut prisms. about 1850. Height 8½ inches.

niques were all copied, so that much that is now classed as foreign was actually made in this country. Many of the surviving pieces are, however, of good but everyday quality and their place of origin is of little importance.

Bohemian skill came to England with the arrival from the late fifties of a number of glass engravers, who took employment at Stourbridge and elsewhere. Emanuel Lerche and Johan Millar or Miller worked in Scottish glass-houses and were responsible for producing, if not introducing, patterns incorporating ferns from about 1862. These plants became immensely popular soon

129

afterwards. Sir Joseph Hooker in 1865 asked Wedgwood's to make some of their jasperware plaques with a pattern of ferns on them to form part of the memorial in Kew Church to his father, Sir W. J. Hooker; and four years later J. S. Hibberd's book, *The Fern Garden,* came out in the first of numerous editions that told its readers how to cultivate for themselves a 'cool grot and mossy cell'. Ferns remained fashionable for at least two further decades, and glassware engraved with their forms was made for another thirty years or more.

At Stourbridge the best-known men who came from Central Europe were William Fritsche, Frederick E. Kny (Fig. 82) and Joseph Keller. All were highly proficient engravers, and examples of their work are to be seen in museums; only occasionally does it appear on the open market. This may be not only on account of its rarity, but because much of it is on a large scale and in a taste that has not at present a wide appeal.

From around 1880 a fresh type of glass-cutting began to be executed, termed *rock-crystal* cutting. The articles to be cut in this style were made with very thick walls, and were carved in the manner of rock-crystal: a revival of the craftmanship of the Renaissance lapidaries who perforce used the natural stone because no suitable imitation then existed. All three of the Stourbridge-based men mentioned above played an important part in creating, as well as filling, public demand for rock-crystal cutting.

Kny and Fritsche both worked for Thomas Webb & Sons, while Keller was with Stevens & Williams. Both firms, in addition, were responsible for the employment of some skilled English workers.

The Portland Vase, the Roman glass vase that is as well known today from Wedgwood jasperware copies as it is for itself, had been for many years in the public eye. The property of successive Dukes of Portland, it had been loaned to the British Museum from 1810 and was displayed there in a glazed case for all to see and admire. For thirty-five years visitors came and went, but at 3.45 p.m. on the 7th February 1845, a scene-painter named William Lloyd picked up a piece of marble standing nearby and smashed both the case and its contents.

The event was a sensational item of news, not only for the wanton damage of a work of art but because of difficulty in applying the law. It was doubted whether Lloyd could be charged with Wilful Damage as the Vase was worth more than £5, so he could

130

Fig. 82
'The Elgin Jug', engraved by F. E. Kny
working for Thomas Webb & Sons, Stourbridge. Exhibited at Paris in 1878. Height
$14\frac{1}{4}$ inches.

be found guilty only of smashing the show-case which was valued at £3. For the crime, to which he confessed, he was fined £3 or two months in prison with hard labour. He possessed no more than ninepence, so the alternative was his lot and to gaol he was sent. In the event, he was there for only two days, as a friend paid the fine and he was released.

The Vase was reduced to over two hundred fragments of various sizes, but a resourceful and patient Museum employee re-assembled them and by September of the same year, a matter of only eight months, it was put on display once more. Thus, a glass masterpiece was suddenly raised from comparative obscurity to being the centre of interest. It was studied more closely than ever before, and the glass-makers of the period duly realised that it represented a challenge to their skill.

Some fifteen years or so after the breaking, the Vase still remained, as far as is known at present, unique and uncopied in its own medium. Then, in 1862, at the International Exhibition held in London was displayed a version of it in glass shown by 'Zach of Munich'. It was sold by auction for £42 later in the same year, and now seems to have disappeared.

A further period of eleven years followed, and in 1873 another craftsman made a determined attempt to emulate the feat of the anonymous Roman. This time it was an Englishman, John North-wood of Stourbridge, whose copy of the Portland Vase occupied him, on and off, three years, until one chilly morning he touched it with a warm hand and it cracked. The mishap was due to the unequal rates of expansion of the two layers of glass, a difficulty that had been overcome eighteen hundred years earlier but one that almost ruined Northwood's work. In spite of the damage he completed his task, and the copy later joined the original in the British Museum.

Cameo glass suddenly became fashionable, and a number of craftsmen soon specialised in it. Webb's of Stourbridge employed the Woodalls, George and Thomas, and the former subsequently stated 'that at one time there were about seventy people assisting my brother and myself in doing this work'. Northwood was also at the head of a large workshop, which became allied to Stevens & Williams, also of Stourbridge. The two firms vied in the produc-tion of ordinary goods for everyday sale as well as costly and sen-sational pieces to gain prestige at exhibitions.

Whereas the Roman cameo-workers relied on the wheel followed by a careful use of steel gravers and files, the Victorians

132

Fig. 83
Copy of the Portland Vase made by
Joseph Locke, who worked for a time in
England and then went to the United
States. 1876. Height 10 inches.

called in chemicals to speed the process. John Northwood's son described how his father proceeded in the following words:

He first draws the design on the opal glass surface and then paints an acid-resisting varnish all over the subject of the

Fig. 84
Plaque of pink glass overlaid with white and carved with Venus and Cupid in a landscape, signed by George Woodall. About 1890. Diameter 16 inches.

design. After the varnish is thoroughly set and firm, the article is immersed in a bath of a mixture of hydrofluoric and sulphuric acids, which dissolves all the opal glass which is unprotected by the varnish, and so allows the transparent coloured under-body to be exposed round the design.

Fig. 85
Vase of yellow glass overlaid with white
and carved with flowers, the whole given a
satin surface. About 1890.

135

Hard steel gravers were used by Northwood, while the Woodalls were aided by copper engraving wheels. These they employed in a variety of diameters, and were able to increase output by their use. In fact, so great was the demand for cameo-glass in its heyday between about 1880 and 1900 that quantity had to be considered above quality. The latter was reserved for specific items designed and made for display to encourage the sale of more ordinary examples.

In contrast to the highly finished cameo pieces there was also a considerable market at the time for blown hand-manipulated wares, in the making of which the ubiquitous cutting-wheel did not play a part. From the days of Henry Cole's short-lived Summerly venture there had been an interest in such productions, and this rapidly increased with the rise to prominence of William Morris and the Arts and Crafts movement he inspired. Earlier in the century there had been a revival at Murano under the leadership of Pietro Bigaglia, and then in the second half of the century came a further renaissance under Antonio Salviati.

The latter revived and augmented the old Venetian styles, in which the molten metal was twisted and shaped, and surfaces fluted, ribbed and decorated with patterned trails of glass 'strings' and 'ribbons'. Contrasting colour was often pale, and the resulting effect completely different from that of cut lead glass.

C. L. Eastlake, a stern critic, writing in 1868 noted that after the middle of the century there had been a change in taste:

People began to discover that the round bulbous form of decanter was a more pleasant object to look at than the rigid outline of pseudo-crystal pint-pot carved and chopped about into unmeaning grooves and planes. The reversed and truncated cone, which served our grandfathers as a model for wine-glasses, gradually disappeared before the lily and crocus-shaped bowls, from which we now sip our sherry and Bordeaux. Champagne had formerly been drunk from tall and narrow glasses, which required to be tossed aloft before they could be emptied. It is now a broad and shallow tazza which sparkles with the vintage of Epernay.

So much for drinking-glasses, and the same applied to most other glass articles; curves were to be seen everywhere, from the well-dressed lady to the glass from which she elegantly sipped her wine. Colour, both pale and harsh, was ubiquitous, and Japanese motifs vied with natural-looking glass branches of cherries, black-

136

Fig. 86
Oil lamps with glass columns and reservoirs, the second example from the right inset with a sulphide head of William Shakespeare. 1820–45.

berries, or unidentifiable flowers. Of all the shades to be found a deep, but transparent, ruby was unquestionably the most popular. Known in the United States as *Cranberry*, it was used for innumerable articles from tumblers to powder-bowls, often with handles or applied frilling in clear glass. Some idea of its vogue can be gained from the fact that for well over a decade it has been crossing the Atlantic literally by the boat-load, and still there is a plentiful supply in English homes.

Considerable skill was exercised in the making of ornamental pieces: particularly vases and bowls for sweetmeats. In the same way as was done with air-twist wine-glass stems, air-bubbles were trapped between two layers of differently coloured glass. The bubbles were then manipulated so as to give a striped or trellis effect in the body of an article, and in many instances it was then finished with a bath of acid to give it a satin surface. Matt finishes were still widely used and appear on all varieties including cameo-

Fig. 87
Four coloured glass bells. Nineteenth
century. Average height 11 inches.

cut, in spite of the fact that the transparency of glass is one of its
beauties.

The popularity of the foregoing kinds of glass coincided with a
fashion for dining by candlelight and for romantically lighting
dark corners of rooms with dim flickerings. Special long-burning
night-lights were placed within domed covers resting on circular
bases, so that the gentle light was enhanced (or not) by the tint
and patterning of the glass. The most novel, and nowadays most
sought after, of the shades are those made by Webb's in what they
called 'Queen's Burmese Ware' : a matt-surfaced glass fading from
a rich pink to a lemon yellow. It originated in the United States,
and was made and marketed in England by the Stourbridge firm.

Glass played a part also in connexion with oil-lighting, and
columns and reservoirs were made in the material (Fig. 86). Glass
shades were, of course, essential, and in some instances the much-
admired ruby was used for them (Plate 15).

As mentioned on an earlier page, friggers of eighteenth-century
types continued to be made and differ little, if at all, from earlier
examples. Although generally allocated to Nailsea, which closed in
1873, they were all over the country and it is rarely possible to be
certain where a specimen originated.

138

7. Bottles

The early type of glass, made by the forest workers from local ingredients, was of a greenish tint because it was not decolourised. Once people had seen the clear Venetian product they naturally preferred it for most purposes, but it was more expensive and for everyday use the green variety was adequate. Articles for medical purposes, such as phials and urinals, were made in large numbers, as were commonplace domestic wares.

The account book of William More, who lived at Loseley, Surrey, records that in 1556 he possessed the undermentioned glass, which was probably of forest make:

25 glasses for waters	5s.
1 great bottle glass	6d.
2 glasses for conserves	4d.
2 other little glasses	1d.
a little glass for water	1d.
a little glass for aqua composita	1d.
2 beer glasses	4d.
2 glasses for waters	4d.

In addition, he possessed other articles, such as '3 glasses like chalices', which were entered at 1s.

Examples of such wares have been excavated. They are of simple shapes, strictly utilitarian and without ornamentation. Their

139

patterns changed little, if at all, with the passing of time, so it is only very rarely possible to date them. This can usually only be done by referring to coins or anything else found with the glass, or by calculations based on the depth from which recovery is made.

Glass of this kind is of limited interest to collectors, and in any case is understandably scarce. Of a wider appeal are the bottles that began to be made from about the middle of the seventeenth century for the purpose of holding wine. Not only are they of more pleasing shapes but they are larger in size and more decorative. In addition, many of the surviving examples are *sealed,* i.e. they bear a glass disc with the name, initials, crest, or coat of arms of the original owner, and frequently also a date.

The glass seal, which averages about an inch in diameter, often enables a bottle to be traced to its original owner. In cases where only initials are present this is not always possible, but in many instances a man used his surname, and added the name of his house, village or town. Thus, a bottle sealed R. NEWMAN 1723, dredged out of the mud in the river Dart, in Devon, once belonged to Robert Newman, a Dartmouth merchant and several times mayor of the town. Other members of the same family, who were connected with the wine trade, put their names to their bottles, and many remain with their descendants. Alternatively, a query is raised with a bottle sealed B L LYME, which might refer to a member of the Leigh family, who lived at Lyme Park, near Stockport, Lancashire, or it could have come from Lyme Regis, in Dorset.

Some of the Oxford colleges had their own bottles, and those with the letter MAG. COLL. C.R. on them came from Magdalen College Common Room. All Souls' College, in the same city, was abbreviated in a similar manner to A.S.C.R., while Lincoln College used a shortened version of the name both with and without its crest, a pair of antlers.

Crests and coats of arms include those of a number of noble families, which are normally not too difficult to identify. A seal with the arms of Earl Poulett, who died in 1743, was found in Taunton, Somerset, while a gas main was being laid, and another was excavated in Williamsburg, Virginia. As the family seat was not far from Taunton the presence there of the seal is easily explained, but how one got to America is at present a mystery.

A further category of seals comprises those made for taverns, which bottled wine on their premises and served it there in their own bottles. Amongst them is that of Ralph and Joan Flexney, who used their initials, RTF and a figure of a bear, at the Bear Inn, Oxford, on the site of which it was found. In the same way W. VINER with a pattern of vine leaves and grapes was placed on the bottles of William Viner, of the Vine Inn, Salisbury, Wiltshire.

Very many more seals have been recorded and identified, and plenty remain for further research. The only book devoted to the subject is that written by the late Lady Ruggles-Brise (S. Ruggles-Brise, *Sealed Bottles,* published in 1949), and articles about them appear from time to time in periodicals. In the United States, Ivor Noël Hume, Director of the Department of Archaeology at Colonial Williamsburg, has written articles and books dealing with the bottles, sealed and plain, that reached America, mostly from England, in the seventeenth and eighteenth centuries.

The use of bottles, as an alternative to a large wooden cask, for the storage and transport of wine is said to have been the idea of Sir Kenelm Digby, a man of varied talents who died in 1665. At about that date it was stated that he had 'invented' wine-bottles and had had some made in 1632. Whether he was concerned in this or not has never been proved, but it is certain that if he had not had the happy thought it would have occurred to someone else.

The bottles that may have been made for Sir Kenelm have disappeared, and there is every probability that if they had lasted for three centuries they would not be distinguishable from others. So far as is known he was not in any way connected with the custom of sealing a bottle, only with providing it with a new use. The adding of a seal was only the revival of a much earlier practice that, like so much else in glass-making, had been current in Roman times.

Bottles, whole or imperfect, dating from the mid-seventeenth century have been preserved. Of some, only the seals have endured, the remainder being so smashed as to be worthless. As with other types of glass, the broken pieces were re-usable in making new articles, and green cullet was sought just as eagerly as flint. This fact explains why old bottles are so scarce, and it may be considered remarkable that under the circumstances all of them were not re-melted. Presumably this would have occurred if some had not been accidentally or deliberately buried or forgotten.

Premeditated concealment of bottles did occasionally take place in connexion with witchcraft, although this usually involved the use of small-sized phials. Wine-bottles were, however, sometimes pressed into service for holding unpleasant concoctions, pins and bits of the flesh of reptiles and animals. Accompanied by suitable spells, the bottles were then buried or otherwise hidden to the discomfiture of the unknowing victim against whom a spell was directed.

The earliest datable portion of a bottle so far known is a seal bearing the name *John Jefferson,* the date *1652* and a coat of arms, which is in the London Museum. Perhaps predating this, is a seal excavated on the site of Williamsburg, Virginia, the provincial capital of the state from 1698 until 1779. In 1832 the last of the old building was destroyed by fire, but in recent years the place has been carefully rebuilt and re-named Colonial Williamsburg. The seal in question bears the initials RW, and as it was found in ground which once belonged to a man named Ralph Womersley it is not unreasonable to assume it once held his wine. Two bottles, each bearing the same R W seal, were found in London some years ago, and it has been suggested that they were also made for Ralph Womersley. As he died in 1651, the bottles and seal could be the earliest surviving specimens.

The Womersley bottles and seal are undated, and the earliest dated complete bottle is five years later, 1657, than the seal in the London Museum. It was found at Wellingborough, Northamptonshire, and is now in the Northampton Museum (Fig. 88). The seal is initialled RMP above a man's head, perhaps that of King Charles I, so it has been conjectured that it was made for the owners of a tavern named The King's Head. As the initials are arranged in a triangle, with the P above the other two letters, they would stand for a man and wife: the topmost being the surname, and the others the forenames of each. For example, $_J{}^S{}_M$ would be used for John and Mary Smith.

From about the middle of the seventeenth century onwards dated bottles are known for most years, and a study of them has shown that their shape changed from time to time. They were placed in convenient categories many years ago by the late W. A. Thorpe, who arranged them as follows:

Circa 1650: the shaft-and-globe—with a globular body and a long neck, rather like a candle stuck in a ball. (Fig. 88)

Circa 1690: the onion—with a short neck emerging from a squat body. (Fig. 89)

142

Fig. 88
Bottle sealed with a King's head, initials
RPM and dated 1657. Found at Welling-
borough and now in the Central Museum,
Northampton. Height 8¾ inches.

Fig. 89
Bottle with a seal inscribed *Cha. Turner*
1690. Height 5$\frac{9}{10}$ inches.

Circa 1715: the slope-and-shoulder—with neck about equal in height to the body, and the latter having almost straight sides sloping inwards and a well-defined shoulder. (Fig. 91)

Circa 1750: the cylinder: forerunner of the present bottle. At first the body was of larger diameter than in modern versions.

All the dates given are approximately those by which the type is usually clearly recognisable. In each instance there was a gradual change from one to the next and, inevitably, there are some bottles

Fig. 90
A row of early eighteenth-century bottles sealed as follows: (*left to right*) G. Burdon, Surscott; J. Whitehorn, Charlton; ditto; unsealed.

quite outside the normal. Among them are those of oval, instead of round shape, and others that are similarly unusual in having three or more flat sides.

The transition from a squat, dumpy bottle to one of tall, cylindrical shape has been largely attributed to the Methuen Treaty of 1703. This was concluded with Portugal, and gained its name from that of the British Ambassador who negotiated and signed it. By its provisions English woollen goods were admitted into Portugal at a preferential rate, while in return the wines of that country came into England at a lower duty than the wines of France.

145

Fig. 91
Two sealed bottles, named and dated as
follows: (*left*) Ann Eilheringtn, 1708,
height 5½ inches; (*right*) James Oakes,
Bury, 1771, height 10¾ inches.

146

It was not long before Portuguese wine, and port was the principal one, began to drive claret and other long-standing favourites from English tables. In due course, too, the virtues of storing a wine and allowing it to mature in the bottle became appreciated, and this applied particularly to port. To store it satisfactorily it was essential that the contents remained completely airtight, and if the bottle was placed so as to allow the wine to keep the cork moist and swollen all would be well. It could be achieved by placing the dumpy bottle cork downwards, but it was preferable to have a bottle that could lie on its side and occupy less space. The cylindrical bottle provided the perfect answer.

All bottles, until the early nineteenth century, were given a *kick*: the base was pushed upwards to form a cone-shaped depression. This was not so that the wine-merchant could give his clients short measure, but to lift the rough pontil-mark clear of the base. Otherwise the mark would not only make scratches wherever it touched, but the bottle would be unsteady when it was stood upright (Plate 10). The depth of the kick varied from bottle to bottle, but was usually more pronounced in the seventeenth century than later.

Another feature that changed with the years was the *string-rim*. This is a double ring of glass at the top of the neck, so placed and designed that the string or wire securing a cork to seal the contents would grip neatly between the raised loops. When the cork was rammed in flush with the bottle-top and considered to be safe, string was no longer necessary but the rings continued to be a feature. This was partly custom, and partly because of the additional strength the rings gave to the vulnerable end of the neck. In the first half of the nineteenth century the twin bands were merged into a single flat reinforcement.

Judging by the marked prevalence of West Country names and insignia on surviving sealed bottles, it seems possible that they were a speciality of one or more glass-houses in that area. Houghton (see page 61) recorded that there were six makers of bottles 'in and about Bristol' in 1696, while ten others were active in Devon, Somerset, Gloucester and Glamorgan. Houghton notes makers in many other parts of the country, but it does seem reasonable at any rate to suppose that bottles with West Country associations on their seals would have been supplied locally.

The bottles were made on the blow-pipe, the body being blown and the neck drawn out from it. When of a sufficient size and correct shape, the pontil was stuck to the base, the blow-pipe broken away and the neck, after being re-heated at the mouth of the kiln, carefully finished. Then the pontil was removed, and the mark made by it pushed up clear of the base. Finally, the finished article was taken away for annealing.

With a continuing heavy demand for bottles it is certain that there was every inducement to find ways of making them more quickly and more cheaply. As early as 1752 a newspaper paragraph mentioned the loss by theft in Bristol of 'one brass Bottle-Mould value 18s.' However, it was not until about seventy years later that Henry Ricketts, a prominent glass-maker in that city, successfully began to mould bottles in quantity. Each bears the wording H. RICKETTS & CO. GLASSWORKS BRISTOL under the base, and PATENT on the shoulder.

The great advantages of moulding were not confined to price and quantity, but the process enabled a more or less perfect uniformity to be achieved. Hitherto, size and shape relied very largely on the eye of the maker, with the use of templates to assist, but now each bottle was reasonably close in capacity to that of its fellows. Seals continued to be used, but not as much as before, and were still applied in the same manner. By about 1840 they had gone out of fashion, but they have been revived in the present century as a trade-mark by some vintners. The modern practice is to mould bottle and seal in a single operation, but comparison between old and new examples will quickly show how one is distinct from the other.

During the eighteenth century many liquids were stored and transported in large square-shaped bottles. Their thin sides were vulnerable, and they were normally kept in boxes or cases. Often known as *case-bottles,* they are made of the same green-coloured glass as contemporaneous wine-bottles. In most instances their sides slope so that the base is smaller than the shoulder, making it a simple matter to remove the blown article from the mould.

The simple phial for medicines was also moulded with lettering. Such popular cure-alls as *Daffy's Elixir, Godfrey's Cordial* and *Turlington's Balsam of Life* were among the much-advertised remedies sold in distinctively marked containers. Early examples of them are very scarce, but many such panaceas continued to be sold until well into Queen Victoria's reign, and were put up in bottles of somewhat similar pattern to those of their first appearance on the market.

A further use of sealed bottles was for holding medicinal waters from both English and foreign spas. Water was brought from

Pyrmont in Germany in bottles datable between 1720 and 1770 with seals of the usual type bearing the words PIERMONT WATER or PYRMONT WATER. Another popular resort of the time was Pouhon-in-Spa, in Belgium, whence came water in bottles sealed with the name of the place and a coat of arms. One of these bottles was found in the wall of a Wiltshire house, and both varieties of the Pyrmont seal have been unearthed across the Atlantic, in Colonial Williamsburg, Virginia.

In a similar fashion, water from Bristol Hotwells was despatched in locally made bottles, which were advertised in the early 1720's at 2s. per dozen empty. At about the same date a writer noted:

... great numbers of bottles, even such as is almost incredible, are now used for sending the waters of St. Vincent's Rock away, which are now carried, not only all over England only, but, we may say, all over the world.

No sealed Bristol-water bottles have yet been found, so it would seem possible that plain containers with a paper label were employed.

A guide for visitors to Bristol, published in 1793, shows that the numerous glass-houses were an attraction to be visited by tourists, and that the bottling of the waters continued. The description written by the anonymous compiler was as follows:

The great demand for glass bottles for the Bristol Water, for the exportation of beer, cyder and perry; for wine, and for the use of Town and Country, keeps the various bottle houses here constantly at work. The call for window glass at home, at Bath and in the Towns about Bristol; in the Western Counties, Wales and from North to South wherever the Bristol Trade extends, and the great quantities sent to America, employ several houses for this article. Here are likewise two houses, in which are made white or flint glass, and phial bottles. They who are strangers to the working of window glass, and to the blowing of white or flint glass, which is formed into such a variety of modes and forms may gratify their curiosity of observing these curious operations by presenting a small gratuity to the workmen, who living in hot climates are very glad of some suction to moisten their clay.

149

A list of suitable glass-houses, their days and times of operation, was then given, and was doubtless appreciated by those with time on their hands plus the necessary curiosity.

More modern waters, man-made in this instance, with a gaseous content to increase their attraction, were sold at one time in ingeniously designed bottles. Each was given a constricted neck within which was a loose glass ball, and a rubber washer at the

Fig. 92
Aerated-drink bottle with captive glass-ball seal made by Dan Rylands, Barnsley, Yorkshire. Early twentieth century. Length 9 inches.

inside of the open end. When the bottle was full, the pressure of gas pushed the ball up against the washer and effectively sealed it. To release the contents, a small wooden cap with a central raised dowel was pressed against the top of the ball, forcing it away from the rubber and releasing the liquid (Fig. 92). Many a lad tried to manage without the wooden cap and so bruised a finger-tip or broke a nail, while even more smashed an empty bottle to get the ball out. When obtained it made an excellent marble for the game of that name.

Bottles of the ball-stopper type were in use as late as the

150

1930s, and many of them were made in Yorkshire. Most bear the name of the maker of their contents in raised letters, and also that of the bottle-maker. The example in Fig. 92 was made by Dan Rylands, Barnsley, Yorkshire.

By the close of the nineteenth century, machines for bottle-making had been developed on both sides of the Atlantic, and were rapidly replacing old-fashioned methods. Expanding populations demanded an ever-increasing supply of cheap bottles, and at the same time insisted on a high standard of accuracy as regards their capacity. Automatic machinery, which incorporated compressed air for blowing, ensured that such a standard was attained, while later research has resulted in more durable types of glass to withstand careless and constant handling.

Bottles of most ages and varieties are collected keenly in all parts of the world, and numerous magazines dealing with antiques in general devote space to the subject. Variations in pattern are traced and dated, and country of origin and maker determined whenever possible. Memories are very short, and a bottle of fifty years ago will sometimes present just as much of a problem as one made in 1700. Habits change quickly, and it may not be many decades before the still-commonplace milk bottle no longer appears daily on city doorsteps, but will have to be sought in a display cabinet.

8. Irish Glass

The history of glass-making in Ireland followed a somewhat similar course to that in England, and the two countries formed a temporary alliance between about 1780 and 1825. The years of partnership resulted in the making of many outstanding pieces of ware, and also gave rise to a considerable amount of misinformation. This has become almost as legendary as the leprechaun, and with just about as much basis of fact.

Almost contemporary with Laurence Vitrearius of Chiddingfold was William the Glassmaker, who is recorded as being granted some land in Dublin in 1258. Other names occur in documents, such as William le Verrir and Richard Glazewright, all of whom probably specialised in the making of sheet glass but would no doubt also have produced phials and other small containers.

The establishment of the industry really dates from 1586, when a retired Army officer, Captain Thomas Woodhouse, was informed that:

Her Majesty considering that the making of glass might prove commodious to both realms and that Woodhouse was the first that with any success had begun the art in Ireland is pleased to condescend to his petition and therefore orders that a grant be made to him of the privilege of making glass for glazing and drinking or otherwise, and to build convenient houses, for the term of eight years. . . .

Within three years he sold his privilege to an Englishman, George Longe, who was already operating a number of glass-houses in his native land. In 1589 Longe addressed a petition drawing the attention of Lord Burghley, then Lord High Treasurer and Queen Elizabeth's principal minister, to the serious depletion of English woodlands by the activities of glass-makers. He suggested a reduction in the number of his glass-houses and their transfer to Ireland, where there was an ample supply of timber. He pointed out that such a move would not only increase employment in that country, but if the forests were reduced there would then be less cover for the numerous rebels they were sheltering.

Longe was granted the permission he sought, and set up a glass-house at Curryglas, in County Cork. The venture would seem to have lasted for about eight years, and is presumed to have resulted in the making of sheet-glass and vessels of coarse types. That he had some success is based in part on a mention in a document of 1597, which includes the words 'George Longe who first brought glass-making to Ireland'.

Other glass-makers came and went throughout the seventeenth century, and there are records of enterprises, mostly small ones, in many counties. Among them was a venture conducted by the Earl of Cork at Ballynagerah, in County Waterford, which was commenced in about 1620, and another that began soon after-wards at Birr, near Dublin.

Not long after George Ravenscroft had devised and patented his flint or lead glass, its manufacture began in Ireland. The first man to make it was a Captain Philip Roche who, with two partners, Richard and Christopher Fitzsimons, took over an exist-ing glass-house in Dublin for the purpose. The premises were known as the Round Glasshouse, and it remained in the owner-ship of a Fitzsimons descendant until about 1760. Just prior to that year, advertisements announced the fact that the proprietor was the only manufacturer of flint glass in Ireland, and that his patterns as well as his craftsmen came from London, and that he could supply 'wine-glasses with a vine border, toasts or any flourish whatsoever'.

This last phrase has been taken to imply that the Round Glass-house was the source of many of the commemorative pieces with Williamite emblems and inscriptions. Dubliners and others held annual festivals in memory of the Battle of the Boyne and the birthday of William III, on 1st July and 4th November respec-

153

tively. Whether any or all the surviving glasses which were made for use on these occasions were made in Dublin or elsewhere in Ireland, or were engraved there, remains a point that is keenly debated.

At about the same date, 1752, the Round Glasshouse listed the goods it was about to supply, which included:

the newest-fashioned drinking-glasses, water-bottles, claret and Burgundy ditto, decanters, jugs, water-glasses [forerunners of finger bowls] with and without feet and saucers, plain, ribbed, and diamond-moulded jelly-glasses of all sorts and sizes, sillybub-glasses, comfit- and sweetmeat-glasses for desserts, salvers, glass plates for china dishes . . .

Although it was to be assumed that all these articles were made on the premises, there is no proof that this was the case. Many of the goods were probably imported from England, and no distinction was made between them and whatever might have been of Dublin make. It was common business practice at a time when, for example, the term 'potter' was applied equally to a man who manufactured goods and to one who merely retailed the work of others.

A few other glass-houses were in existence in Dublin for short periods, but in 1745 the Irish manufacturers were forbidden by law to export any of their ware. They were forced to rely solely on home sales, and their output was thereby severely limited. The Act left the country more or less at the mercy of English makers, who could easily undersell the few struggling local glass-houses.

The latter were encouraged, as far as possible, by monetary grants awarded by the Royal Dublin Society, counterpart of the London-based Society for the Encouragement of Arts and Manufactures (now the Royal Society of Arts). The Dublin body, which enjoyed Government assistance, disbursed the sum of £42,000 between 1761 and 1767, but only a proportion of this went towards assisting glass-makers.

Of these, the firm of Richard Williams & Co., of Marlborough Green, Dublin, was granted £1,600 in 1764. With its aid they were able to assure their customers nine years later that they 'had brought the manufacture to as great perfection as carried on abroad'. In proof of this, in 1777 they erected a new glass-house in Marlborough Street, and continued to trade for a further period of half a century.

The success of the Williams firm was the more remarkable be-

154

cause it was achieved against a background of trade depression. The Americans and British had been quarrelling for a decade when, finally, on 19th April 1775, at Lexington, Massachusetts, the War of Independence broke out. Just over twelve months later the Declaration of Independence was approved and signed, and was

Fig. 93
Fruit or salad bowl cut with large diamonds, the rim castellated and the foot of 'lemon-squeezer' pattern. About 1785. Width 12 inches.

followed by the alliance of the French with the fledgling United States.

There was then a possibility that French troops might invade Ireland and attack the British. A volunteer defence force was raised, and within a short time some 40,000 Irishmen had been recruited. The Dublin politicians were not slow to see their opportunity and, led by the eloquent Henry Grattan, as a condition of their loyalty they clamoured to be allowed to trade with whom they pleased. The London Parliament could hardly

155

resist the call, and in 1780 enacted legislation which allowed the Irish the same facilities as had been for long enjoyed by the British.

The Act of 1745 which prohibited Irish exports of glass also laid a tax on British production, but left Ireland's glass-houses completely untouched in that respect. Thus, when free trade was at last granted in 1780 there was every hope that it would prove of benefit. Slightly earlier, in 1777, the English had increased their own tax, and then raised it further in 1781. This last turn of the screw provided the impetus, the attraction of Ireland as a manufacturing base became irresistible and there began a migration to the tax-free haven.

By the end of the century, the industry had established itself so well that a commentator wrote of it:

> At present we are able not only to supply our home consumption but to export very considerable quantities to America and elsewhere. Much of the glassware consumed in Ireland is imported, for our houses find the supply of the American market so much more lucrative and have so much of that trade that they think lightly of supplying the home consumption. The houses of this city [Dublin] which are in the American trade have generally orders for New York sufficient to occupy them entirely for two years. The principal materials are imported from England, though we are able to undersell the British manufacturer.

Certainly, a considerable change had taken place within no more than a couple of decades, and the principal firms which shared in this rise in fortune will now be considered.

WATERFORD

It has been mentioned earlier that there was a glass-house in Waterford early in the seventeenth century, but like so many others it was short-lived. It is the factory of more recent date that has made the name of the city synonymous with Irish glass, and given it an enduring fame. A brief announcement in the *Dublin Evening Post* of 4th October 1783 informed the public of the start of activities. It ran:

> Waterford Glass House. George and William Penrose have established an extensive glass manufacture in this city; their

156

friends and the public may be supplied with all kinds of plain and flint glass, useful and ornamental.

The Penrose brothers were wealthy Waterford merchants, and their venture into glass-making depended on the knowledge of a Stourbridge man, John Hill. He brought with him what was stated to have been 'the best set of workmen that he could get in the

Fig. 94
Bowl cut with a pattern of flat diamonds and leaves, the rim scalloped and the square foot moulded on the inside. About 1790. Width 12 inches.

county of Worcester'. A month after they had opened their warehouse the Penroses sought and obtained a grant from the Government, and three years later attempted the same again. It is not known whether the second attempt was successful, but in any case the business progressed satisfactorily.

John Hill had been an important manufacturer prior to his arrival in Ireland, and his employment at Waterford gave the factory a good start. Regrettably, in 1786, only three years after his coming, he hurriedly left. It would seem he was not only un-

157

popular with the Irish employees, but he somehow offended the wife of one of the Penroses, who accused him of unseemly behaviour. In a sad note which he left addressed to his friend and confidant, Jonathan Gatchell, he wrote beseeching him 'For heaven's sake do not reproach me but put the best construction on my conduct'.

He had fortunately communicated to Gatchell all the manufacturing secrets learned at Stourbridge, and applied with such success at Waterford. With this vital knowledge, Gatchell, although employed in the capacity of a clerk, quickly rose in the firm, until in 1799 he became a partner. Finally, he was in sole charge up to 1823, when he died and there followed further changes in the composition of the company.

The glass made at Waterford has been the subject of lengthy argument. Principally this has concerned the alleged blue tint by which it can be distinguished, and which it was firmly stated was exclusive to that glass. The 'dark bluish-black' shade was most certainly not confined to glass from the Waterford factory where, as a matter of fact, a note in the Gatchell papers stresses that the firm made every endeavour to produce a metal that was clear and white. A grey-blue is found in the glass from many sources, and a number of explanations have been put forward to account for its presence. Not only is it attributable to an excess of decolouriser (oxide of manganese) or to impurities in the various constituents, but it has been suggested that it can appear as a result of atmospheric action.

A small proportion of the output from Waterford was marked, and this comprises mostly decanters. Each bears running round the underside of the base in slightly raised letters the words PENROSE WATERFORD. It has been pointed out that the decanters have a number of recognisable features, which are:

1 A mushroom-shaped stopper cut with radial flutes and with the top resting on a rounded knop.
2 The top of the neck has a wide flat rim.
3 The neck bears three plain triple rings.
4 Cutting comprises areas of fine diamonds, or else a band of strawberry diamonds below a ring of arrow-heads.
5 The base is moulded with vertical flutes about two inches in height.

The late W. A. Thorpe, who noted the above details, added a word of warning: 'There is no proof that decanters which exhibit these

158

features are Waterford or that those which do not are not.' It should be added that the lettering, when present, is not always readily discovered, as it is often far from clear. Also, understandably in view of their rarity and the great demand for examples, marked specimens have been faked.

The fame of Waterford, and of Irish glass in general, rests on its

Fig. 95
Bowl cut with upright flutes and semi-circular swags, the rim shaped and the whole raised on a square stepped foot. About 1790. Width 15 inches.

cutting. Absence of tax meant that there was no limit to the amount of actual glass forming a piece, it could be made as heavy as desired without causing the price to be prohibitive and the cutter could give full play to his fancy. Also, in spite of the duty, closely similar work was being executed at the time in England, and as the majority of the craftsmen in Ireland were immigrants it is quite impossible in most instances to be certain of the origin of a specimen.

Often attributed to Waterford, but equally probably the product of any of the other Irish factories, are the large-sized oval or
boat-shaped fruit bowls (Figs. 94 to 96). Each is raised on a short
stem above a circular or a square foot, the latter often moulded
with radial ribs. It is sometimes termed a 'lemon-squeezer foot'

Fig. 96
Bowl cut with upright fluting and a band
of leaves, the rim shaped and bevelled
and the foot of 'lemon-squeezer' type.
About 1800. Width 12¼ inches.

because of its close resemblance to that useful piece of domestic
equipment.

The bowls, which are very heavily constructed with thick sides,
sometimes have the upper edge curved outwards and are known
sometimes as *turn-over* bowls (Fig. 97). Their ornamentation em-
braced every variety of cut, which was given careful polishing to
ensure a high standard of finish. Among the more remarkable
features was the *step cut*, comprising a series of parallel ridges

160

reflecting light in a distinctive brilliant manner. Step-cutting requires a considerable mass of glass for its execution, and was at the height of its popularity between about 1815 and 1820.

Following the death of Jonathan Gatchell in 1823, the factory,

Fig. 97
Bowl with turned-over rim cut with short vertical flutes, the knopped stem rising from a 'lemon-squeezer' foot. About 1790. Width about 12 inches.

as well as the entire Irish industry, suffered a further blow in 1825 when the Dublin government introduced a tax on glass. Within a short time production dropped, and the earlier prosperity was never recovered. Gone were the days when Cork shipped as many as 104,720 drinking glasses to Jamaica (1801), or when Dublin exported 205,200 to New York (1810).

Waterford did its best to carry on, and its then proprietor,

George Gatchell, displayed a selection of the firm's products at the Great Exhibition in 1851. According to the catalogue he showed:

Etagère, or ornamental centre stand for a banqueting table; consisting of forty pieces of cut glass, so fitted to each other as to require no connecting sockets of any other material. Quart and pint decanters, cut in hollow prisms. Centre vase, or bowl, on detached tripod stand. Vases with covers.

Alas, the firm did not outlast the Exhibition, and a month before it closed was advertising a sale of 'the entire stock of glass'. On 23rd December 1851, Gatchell left Ireland and made his home in Bristol, and not long afterwards the contents of the glass-house and cutting-shop were sold. In recent years a new company has been formed, and successfully makes wares in the old styles.

CORK

In 1783, the same year as operations commenced at Waterford, the Cork Glass Company established a glass-house in Hanover Street. Financial difficulties would appear to have dogged the proprietors, who suspended business in 1787 and petitioned the Government for a grant. They received an award of £1,600, but in spite of it there were continuing changes of partners until the firm ceased trading in 1818.

Just prior to the closure at Hanover Street, a glass-dealer named Daniel Foley opened the Waterloo Glass House Company, with its manufactory on Wandesford Quay. In 1816 the *Cork Overseer* informed its readers of what was in store for them in the following terms:

Foley's workmen are well selected, from whose superior skill the most beautiful glass will shortly make its appearance to dazzle the eyes of the' public, and to outshine those of any competitor. He is to treat his men at Christmas with a whole roasted ox and everything adequate. They have a new band of music with bassoon serpents, horns, trumpets, etc., and they have a glass pleasure boat, a cot and a glass set which when seen will astonish the world.

There is no record of the effect of these promised wonders, only mentions of Foley retiring in 1830 and of the company going bankrupt five years afterwards.

A third Cork company was established by two brothers, Edward and Richard Ronayne, in South Terrace. The Terrace Glass Works

162

opened in 1819, and possibly hoped to profit by the very recent demise of the Waterloo Company. This could have been achieved by employing some of their craftsmen and by attracting some of their customers, but it is not known whether either or both occurred. The brothers dissolved their partnership in 1838, and the business was closed three years later.

Two of the firms made decanters and, as at Waterford and else-

Fig. 98
Water jugs, the body of each partly moulded with shallow flutes and engraved: marked (*left*) CORK GLASS CO.; (*right*) WATERLOO CO. CORK. About 1810 and 1820.

where, marked them with their names beneath the bases. Most specimens have the typical Irish triple rings round the neck, a mushroom-shaped stopper and upright flutes round the lower part of the body. Those marked CORK GLASS CO can have two, three or four neck-rings, as opposed to the almost constant three of others, and the rings are often *feathered* or moulded with tiny vertical ridges. Especially common to Cork is cutting in the form of a series of vesicas: ovals with pointed ends. Of the Terrace Glass

163

Fig. 99
Irish decanters and stoppers, marked
(*outside pair*) CORK GLASS CO.; (*left
centre*) unmarked; (*right centre*) WATER-
LOO CO. CORK. About 1800. Average
height 10 inches.

Works no marked productions have been recorded, nor is it
known whether they made wares in any particular style.

BELFAST

A Bristol glass-maker, Benjamin Edwards, came to Ireland in
1771 and established a glass-works near Dungannon, County
Tyrone. After a few years he moved to Belfast and set up the Long
Bridge Glass-House which, with numerous vicissitudes and a
change of address, remained in operation until the mid-nineteenth
century. Again, marked decanters are known, this time with B
EDWARDS under the base, and with the usual moulded fluting.
Perhaps because he is known to have employed a number of
Bristol workers, the decanters are of the tall tapering shape that
was produced in West Country glass-houses. Unlike many of those
made elsewhere in Ireland, the rim at the mouth is quite narrow,
the rings round the neck are usually two in number and of a simple
triangular section, while the stoppers are upright of round or
lozenge shape with bevelled or fluted edges.

164

Drawn-stem: Wine-glass with the stem drawn out from the base of the bowl and therefore composed of two parts. Compare with *Stuck-stem.*

Enamel: Specially compounded colours applied in the same manner as oil-paints and then fired to fix them permanently. Also used as a name for opaque white glass resembling porcelain.

Flint-glass: See *Lead-glass.*

Frigger: A piece of glassware made by a worker in his spare time, but often applied to such articles as model ships, bells and walking sticks, which are more surprising than they are practical.

Frit: Materials part-melted, to be ground-up for incorporation in the batch.

Gadget: A variety of puntee with a spring-clip to grip articles, and therefore not leaving a mark where it was used.

Gadroons: Lobes or ribs, usually radiating, sometimes used as ornament.

Gaffer: A principal craftsman in a glass-house.

Glory-hole: A small-sized opening in the side of the glass furnace.

Kick: The conical depression under an article, formed to raise the pontil-mark so that it did not damage a surface and allowed the article to stand firmly upright. Applied particularly to wine-bottles.

Knop: A bulge, either solid or hollow, in the stem of a vessel.

Lead-glass: Glass of which a constituent is oxide of lead, devised by the Englishman George Ravenscroft and known also as flint-glass.

Leer: An annealing oven. A tunnel through which the finished glass articles are drawn slowly on iron trolleys from the hot end to the cool.

169

Marver: An iron or marble slab on which the paraison was rolled to shape and smooth it.

Merese: A sharp-edged button between the bowl and the stem of a wine-glass.

Metal: The glass material itself, either in molten or cold form.

'Nipt diamond waies': Used by George Ravenscroft to describe a raised diamond-shaped ornament employed on some of the productions of his own glass-house and of others.

Paraison: The lump of molten glass on the end of a blowing-iron.

Pontil or *Puntee:* An iron rod with which to hold an article during manufacture.

Pontil-mark, alternatively *Puntee-mark:* The rough scar left where the pontil or puntee was broken away.

Prunt: A flat blob of glass, often moulded with a strawberry pattern, applied to the stem or the bowl of a glass either as ornament or to provide a hand-grip.

Purlee: A term used by George Ravenscroft, probably to describe a raised pattern of small dots.

Silesian stem: A faceted stem with well-defined shoulders, sometimes moulded with initials or a short inscription.

Straw Stem: See *Drawn-stem.*

String-rim: The rings round the top of the neck of a wine bottle, provided to take the string or wire holding the cork in place.

Stuck-stem: Wine-glass with the stem composed of three parts joined together in the making: bowl, stem and foot.

Tear: A single entrapped air-bubble, often the shape of a teardrop which gave it its name, found in the stems of wine-glasses, the bases of bowls and elsewhere.

Threading: Thin strands of glass applied round an article for ornament.

170

Index

171

173